יהוה

To

Be

Erect

By: תמר שראי ישראל

יהוה

To Be Erect

They shall not hurt nor destroy in all my holy mountain: for the earth shall be full of the knowledge of the LORD יהוה, as the waters cover the sea. Isaiah 11:9 KJV

By: תמר שראי ישראל

Table Of Contents

Dedication

This book is dedicated to the spiritual resurrection of the righteous people of the Earth and to the establishment of the Kingdom of Shalom--the Kingdom of God, יהוה.

Acknowledgement

I will forever thank my Father, יהוה for giving me the opportunity to put this book together. I pray every one of you reading this book has it in your hearts to want to learn, love and follow Abba יהוה. There is no greater love or blessing than his. May Abba יהוה guide you, protect you and keep you. I want you to know that יהוה loves you and if you love him you will do as John 14:15 KJV.

Introduction

Shalom Aleichem, I am excited to bring this knowledge to the forefront for your consideration. The word "erect" has many different meanings. My name is Tamar and it is Hebrew, as am I. Tamar means "to be erect; palmtree". When I first came across this word, I automatically thought, "something upright or standing tall". But, when we think about it, what does it mean to be erect? I will further explain so that you have a better understanding. The word erect in Hebrew is *Natsab* (נצב), found in Strong's Concordance No. 5324; it means: a prim root; to station, in various applications (literally or figuratively):--appointed, deputy, erect, establish, × Huzzah (by mistake for a proper name), lay, officer, pillar, present, rear up, set (over, up), settle, sharpen, establish, (make to) stand(-ing, still, up, upright), best state. We can conclude from this definition that erect means to be not leaning nor bending but straightforward, perpendicular, and reared upwards. Yahweh wants us to be literally perfect in every way, shape and form. If someone is dishonest, it means they are not being erect or projecting the characteristics Yahweh demands from us. To be erect means we will behave and live out our lives in a moral sense. When the world wakes up and realizes that being erect is possible, there will be no need for law enforcement. To be erect is a gateway for every soul on this Earth to do what is right by being righteous. Yahweh put laws in place that are perfect but Man chooses to do as they please. Free will is a gift from Yahweh. We have a choice in this waking life. Everyday we get a chance to do the right thing. I urge you to take this into consideration: Choose to be erect. Doing what is right is not always easy but it sure does give you peace of mind knowing that you made the right choice. Choose to practice charity rather than thievery or deceit. Make a decision to take a stand against corruption. Learn to love yourself when you choose modesty. All the aforementioned attributes and more are great examples of what it means to be erect.

Preface

Before we dive into "to be erect", let's look at some biblical scriptures that mention "upright, raised, pitch, set up and upstanding." found in the Torah. Let us look at scriptures outside the Torah as well, which can be found in the King James Version (**KJV**) Old Testament and New Testament.

See Case Law **§ Psalms 18:25** "With the merciful thou wilt shew thyself merciful; with an upright man thou wilt shew thyself upright"

See Case Law **§ 2 Samuel 22:26** "With the merciful thou wilt shew thyself merciful, and with the upright man thou wilt shew thyself upright"

See Case Law **§ Psalms 7:10** "My defence is of Yahweh, which saveth the upright in heart"

See Case Law **§ Psalms 119:137** "TZADDI. Righteous art thou, O LORD Yahweh, and upright are thy judgments"

See Case Law **§ Psalms 92:15** "To shew that the LORD Yahweh is upright: he is my rock, and there is no unrighteousness in him"

See Case Law **§ Psalms 18:23** "I was also upright before him, and I kept myself from mine iniquity"

See Case Law § **2 Samuel 22:24** "I was also upright before him, and have kept myself from mine iniquity"

See Case Law § **Psalms 25:8** "Good and upright is the LORD Yahweh: therefore will he teach sinners in the way"

See Case Law § **Job 12:4** "I am as one mocked of his neighbour, who calleth upon Yahweh, and he answereth him: the just upright man is laughed to scorn"

See Case Law § **Psalms 11:7** "For the righteous LORD Yahweh loveth righteousness; his countenance doth behold the upright"

See Case Law § **Proverbs 21:29** "A wicked man hardeneth his face: but as for the upright, he directeth his way"

See Case Law § **Proverbs 13:6** "Righteousness keepeth him that is upright in the way: but wickedness overthroweth the sinner"

See Case Law § **Acts 14:10** "Said with a loud voice, Stand upright on thy feet. And he leaped and walked"

See Case Law § **Psalms 94:15** "But judgment shall return unto righteousness: and all the upright in heart shall follow it"

See Case Law § **Psalms 36:10** "O continue thy lovingkindness unto them that know thee; and thy righteousness to the upright in heart"

See Case Law **§ Psalms 32:11** "Be glad in the LORD Yahweh, and rejoice, ye righteous: and shout for joy, all ye that are upright in heart"

See Case Law **§ Habakkuk 2:4** "Behold, his soul which is lifted up is not upright in him: but the just shall live by his faith"

See Case Law **§ Daniel 8:18** "Now as he was speaking with me, I was in a deep sleep on my face toward the ground: but he touched me, and set me upright"

See Case Law **§ Ecclesiastes 7:29** "Lo, this only have I found, that Yahweh hath made man upright; but they have sought out many inventions"

See Case Law **§ Proverbs 29:10** "The bloodthirsty hate the upright: but the just seek his soul"

See Case Law **§ Psalms 37:18** "The LORD Yahweh knoweth the days of the upright: and their inheritance shall be for ever"

See Case Law **§ Job 8:6** "If thou wert pure and upright; surely now he would awake for thee, and make the habitation of thy righteousness prosperous"

See Case Law **§ Psalms 125:4** "Do good, O LORD Yahweh, unto those that be good, and to them that are upright in their hearts"

See Case Law **§ Psalms 112:4** "Unto the upright there ariseth light in the darkness: he is gracious, and full of compassion, and righteous"

See Case Law § **Job 17:8** "Upright men shall be astonied at this, and the innocent shall stir up himself against the hypocrite"

See Case Law § **Proverbs 11:6** "The righteousness of the upright shall deliver them: but transgressors shall be taken in their own naughtiness"

See Case Law § **Proverbs 16:17** "The highway of the upright is to depart from evil: he that keepeth his way preserveth his soul"

See Case Law § **Psalms 112:2** "His seed shall be mighty upon earth: the generation of the upright shall be blessed"

See Case Law § **Proverbs 10:29** "The way of the LORD Yahweh is strength to the upright: but destruction shall be to the workers of iniquity"

See Case Law § **Psalms 20:8** "They are brought down and fallen: but we are risen, and stand upright"

See Case Law § **Psalms 97:11** "Light is sown for the righteous, and gladness for the upright in heart"

See Case Law § **Proverbs 12:6** "The words of the wicked are to lie in wait for blood: but the mouth of the upright shall deliver them"

See Case Law § **Proverbs 11:20** "They that are of a froward heart are abomination to the LORD Yahweh: but such as are upright in their way are his delight."

See Case Law **§ Ecclesiastes 12:10** "The preacher sought to find out acceptable words: and that which was written was upright, even words of truth"

See Case Law **§ Psalms 33:1** "Rejoice in the LORD Yahweh, O ye righteous: for praise is comely for the upright"

See Case Law **§ Proverbs 15:8** "The sacrifice of the wicked is an abomination to the LORD Yahweh: but the prayer of the upright is his delight"

See Case Law **§ Proverbs 11:11** "By the blessing of the upright the city is exalted: but it is overthrown by the mouth of the wicked"

See Case Law **§ Psalms 37:37** "Mark the perfect man, and behold the upright: for the end of that man is peace"

See Case Law **§ Proverbs 29:27** "An unjust man is an abomination to the just: and he that is upright in the way is abomination to the wicked"

See Case Law **§ Proverbs 28:10** "Whoso causeth the righteous to go astray in an evil way, he shall fall himself into his own pit: but the upright shall have good things in possession"

See Case Law **§ Proverbs 2:21** "For the upright shall dwell in the land, and the perfect shall remain in it"

See Case Law **§ Psalms 19:13** "Keep back thy servant also from presumptuous sins; let them not have dominion over me: then shall I be upright, and I shall be innocent from the great transgression"

See Case Law **§ Psalms 140:13** "Surely the righteous shall give thanks unto thy name: the upright shall dwell in thy presence"

See Case Law **§ Micah 7:4** "The best of them is as a brier: the most upright is sharper than a thorn hedge: the day of thy watchmen and thy visitation cometh; now shall be their perplexity"

See Case Law **§ Isaiah 26:7** "The way of the just is uprightness: thou, most upright, dost weigh the path of the just"

See Case Law **§ Proverbs 21:18** "The wicked shall be a ransom for the righteous, and the transgressor for the upright"

See Case Law **§ Proverbs 14:11** "The house of the wicked shall be overthrown: but the tabernacle of the upright shall flourish"

See Case Law **§ Psalms 11:2** "For, lo, the wicked bend their bow, they make ready their arrow upon the string, that they may privily shoot at the upright in heart"

See Case Law **§ Micah 7:2** "The good man is perished out of the earth: and there is none upright among men: they all lie in wait for blood; they hunt every man his brother with a net"

See Case Law **§ Proverbs 11:3** "The integrity of the upright shall guide them: but the perverseness of transgressors shall destroy them"

See Case Law **§ Psalms 37:14** "The wicked have drawn out the sword, and have bent their bow, to cast down the poor and needy, and to slay such as be of upright conversation"

See Case Law **§ Psalms 64:10** "The righteous shall be glad in the LORD Yahweh, and shall trust in him; and all the upright in heart shall glory"

See Case Law **§ Job 1:8** "And the LORD Yahweh said unto Satan, Hast thou considered my servant Job, that there is none like him in the earth, a perfect and an upright man, one that feareth Yahweh, and escheweth evil?"

See Case Law **§ Exodus 15:8** "And with the blast of thy nostrils the waters were gathered together, the floods stood upright as an heap, and the depths were congealed in the heart of the sea"

See Case Law **§ Psalms 111:1** "Praise ye the LORD Yahweh. I will praise the LORD Yahweh with my whole heart, in the assembly of the upright, and in the congregation"

See Case Law **§ Leviticus 26:13** "I am the LORD Yahweh your God, which brought you forth out of the land of Egypt, that ye should not be their bondmen; and I have broken the bands of your yoke, and made you go upright"

See Case Law **§ Jeremiah 10:5** "They are upright as the palm tree, but speak not: they must needs be borne, because they cannot go. Be not afraid of them; for they cannot do evil, neither also is it in them to do good"

See Case Law **§ Daniel 10:11** "And he said unto me, O Daniel, a man greatly beloved, understand the words that I speak unto thee, and stand upright: for unto thee am I now sent. And when he had spoken this word unto me, I stood trembling"

See Case Law **§ Song of Solomon 1:4** "Draw me, we will run after thee: the king hath brought me into his chambers: we will be glad and rejoice in thee, we will remember thy love more than wine: the upright love thee"

See Case Law **§ Job 1:1** "There was a man in the land of Uz, whose name was Job; and that man was perfect and upright, and one that feared Yahweh, and eschewed evil"

See Case Law **§ Genesis 37:7** "For, behold, we were binding sheaves in the field, and, lo, my sheaf arose, and also stood upright; and, behold, your sheaves stood round about, and made obeisance to my sheaf"

See Case Law **§ Psalms 49:14** "Like sheep they are laid in the grave; death shall feed on them; and the upright shall have dominion over them in the morning; and their beauty shall consume in the grave from their dwelling"

See Case Law **§ Daniel 11:17** "He shall also set his face to enter with the strength of his whole kingdom, and upright ones with him; thus shall he do: and he shall give him the daughter of women, corrupting her: but she shall not stand on his side, neither be for him"

See Case Law **§ Job 2:3** "And the LORD Yahweh said unto Satan, Hast thou considered my servant Job, that there is none like him in the earth, a perfect and an upright man, one that feareth Yahweh, and escheweth evil? and still he holdeth fast his integrity, although thou movedst me against him, to destroy him without cause"

See Case Law **§ 2 Chronicles 29:34** "But the priests were too few, so that they could not flay all the burnt offerings: wherefore their brethren the Levites did help them, till the work was ended, and until the other priests had sanctified themselves: for the Levites were more upright in heart to sanctify themselves than the priests"

See Case Law **§ 1 Samuel 29:6** "Then Achish called David, and said unto him, Surely, as the LORD Yahweh liveth, thou hast been upright, and thy going out and thy coming in with me in the host is good in my sight: for I have not found evil in thee since the day of thy coming unto me unto this day: nevertheless the lords favour thee not"

Chapter 1

What does it mean to be erect? It means that an individual is intentional in how they think and behave in their everyday life. It means one will go out of their way to make sure they are being a person who contributes to society in a positive way. To be erect requires a great deal of consistency, commitment, and perseverance. As spiritual beings, we encounter countless situations where tough decisions need to be made. Everyday, life is a challenge and we are tempted to do the unthinkable. The Hebrew word for upright is Tamym (תמים), it means from tamam; entire (literally, figuratively or morally); also (as noun) integrity, truth -- without blemish, complete, full, perfect, sincerely (-ity), sound, without spot, undefiled, upright(-ly), whole. Yahweh wants us to be as perfect as he is, see Case Law **§ Deuteronomy 18:13** "Thou shalt be perfect with the LORD Yahweh thy God". You must decide whether you are going to change for the better. The word תמים (tamym) is used in various backgrounds in the Hebrew Bible, often describing moral integrity, blamelessness, or physical perfection. It is regularly used to describe individuals who are upright or righteous in their endeavors. The society we live in does not push the narrative to be upright, or to follow Yahweh with all your heart, mind, body, and soul. We have the power to change the world based on how we live and treat others. What does it mean to be upright? The word "upright" is a term that carries a rich and meaningful significance, extending beyond its simple definition to embody principles of integrity, morality, and proper posture. To be upright is to embody a sense of moral steadfastness, honesty, and moral rectitude, while also referring to a physical state of being vertically aligned. Understanding what it truly means to be upright involves exploring its literal sense and its figurative implications.

The definition of upright has two primary meanings. The first pertains to physical positioning. When something or someone is "upright," they are standing or positioned vertically, with their body or object aligned perpendicular to the ground. For example, a person standing tall with good posture is considered upright, as is a piece of furniture kept in a vertical position. This physical sense emphasizes stability, balance, and proper alignment. The second more profound meaning of "upright" relates to moral character. In this context, being upright refers to possessing integrity, honesty, and equity. An upright person is someone who consistently adheres to moral principles, acts ethically, and demonstrates honesty even when it is difficult or inconvenient. The moral aspect of the word "upright" implies a sense of inner strength or a person who remains true to their values and principles regardless of external pressures or temptations, for instance. There are a few synonyms for the word "upright". Synonyms for "upright" can vary depending on whether we are considering the physical or moral context.

Physically, synonyms include:

- Vertical
- Erect
- Perpendicular
- Standing
- Verticalized

Morally or ethically, some synonyms are:

- Honest
- Virtuous
- Moral
- Righteous
- Just
- Principled
- Noble
- Upright (itself used as an adjective here)

The common trend among these synonyms is the idea of alignment, either physically or morally, that conveys a sense of correctness, stability, and integrity.

There are numerous antonyms for the word "upright". They differ based on the context used. *Physically*, antonyms include:

- Lying down
- Reclined
- Leaning
- Slouched
- Horizontal

Morally or ethically, antonyms include:

- Dishonest
- Corrupt
- Unprincipled
- Deceitful
- Immoral
- Crooked
- Unethical

The aforementioned antonyms suggest a deviation from stability or moral uprightness, indicating either a physical falling or a lapse in integrity and virtue. We must gain an understanding of what it means to be upright. To be upright, in one sense, is to embody a sense of stability, confidence, and moral clarity. Physically, it indicates healthful posture and strength, standing tall and confident. Figuratively, it represents a commitment to truth, justice, and ethical principles. An upright person is someone others can trust, someone whose actions align with their words, and whose character is marked by honesty and equity. Living uprightly requires conscious effort such as cultivating virtues like honesty, humility, and courage. It means standing firm in one's convictions, even in the face of adversity or temptation. It also involves taking responsibility for one's actions and striving to uphold moral standards, not just for oneself but as a moral example for others. Why does being upright matter? The importance of being upright goes beyond personal integrity. It influences communities and societies. Upright individuals help contribute to society by being trustworthy, respectful, and understanding.

Their actions serve as a foundation for healthy relationships, social cohesion, and justice. Conversely, when people drift away from uprightness such as by becoming dishonest, corrupt, or unjust, the stability of the social fabric is weakened. In a world often filled with challenges and moral ambiguities, choosing to be upright is a conscious decision to prioritize morality and integrity. It's about maintaining a sense of inner balance, standing tall through life's difficulties, and acting in accordance with one's principles. Here is a comprehensive scenario centered on moral character, emphasizing integrity, and designed to inspire individuals to stand up and stand out: In a world that often urges simple- mindedness and sometimes rewards shallowness, the true nature of a person's character is revealed not by fleeting successes or external accolades but by the unwavering strength of their soul. At the heart of this lies integrity which is a virtue that beckons us to stand tall, stand out, and remain true to who we are, regardless of the circumstances. Moral character is the foundation upon which trust is built. It is the steady compass that governs our actions when no one is watching and when the stakes are high. To develop and embody such character is to commit oneself to a life of authenticity, honesty, and ethics. It is a conscious choice to act rightly, not because it is easy or popular, but because it aligns with the deepest principles of who we are and who we aspire to be. Integrity, in particular, is the cornerstone of moral character. It is the attribute that compels us to do what is right even when it is inconvenient, costly, or controversial. Integrity means being honest in our words, sincere in our intentions, and tenacious in our endeavors. It means keeping promises and honoring commitments, even when no one is watching or when doing so might not offer immediate gain. It is a silent but powerful declaration that our principles are more important than selfish desires or superficial success. When we embody integrity, we distinguish ourselves as individuals worthy of honor and respect. We stand out in a crowd not because of boastful displays or superficial charm, but because of a quiet confidence rooted in sincerity and moral conviction. Such people inspire others by leading by example, earning respect not through forced facades but through genuine strength of character. Their lives become a testament to the idea that true greatness is built on moral steadiness and unwavering commitment to doing what is right.

Standing out as a person of moral character requires courage— courage to speak the truth in difficult situations, to own up to mistakes, and to do the right thing even when it is unpopular. Courage demands a willingness to face adversity with humility and resilience. It is important to note that integrity is often tested in moments of challenge. Yet, it is precisely in these moments that our character is truly revealed and explored. By nurturing our moral character, we also influence those around us. Our actions ripple outward, inspiring others to reflect on their own values and to act with integrity. We become beacons of honesty and goodness in a world that desperately needs examples of genuine virtue. By standing firm in our moral convictions, we create a ripple effect, encouraging a society in which honesty, respect, and equity are the norm. Ultimately, standing tall in moral character is about more than just personal virtue. It is about contributing to a better society, living in a way that affirms our dignity and the dignity of others, as well as choosing integrity every day, knowing that our actions define us more than words ever could. Many are tempted to cut corners or compromise on their values for the sake of short- lived gains. Choose instead to stand out by standing up. Let your integrity shine as a guiding light, not just for your own life but as an inspiration for others. Be the person who through unwavering moral character, elevates the standards of honesty and goodness in the world. In the end, demonstrating good character has nothing to do with making easy choices. It deals with doing the right thing regardless of the situation. It's about embodying the noblest aspects of human virtues. And in doing so, we not only define ourselves but also inspire others to do the same. Now, on to the word "encouragement", the power of courage in building moral character. In the journey of life, encouragement is the gentle yet powerful force that sustains us through challenges and uncertainties. It is the compassionate voice that whispers hope in our moments of doubt, reminding us of our inherent strength and worth. When we speak of encouragement, we are also speaking of a vital ingredient in cultivating moral character—a character rooted in integrity, kindness, and resilience. Among the many qualities that define true moral strength, courage stands out as perhaps the most essential. It is the brave heart that refuses to give up, even when the road is tough, and the right path seems difficult to follow.

Courage is not the absence of fear, rather, it is the willingness to face our fears head-on and act rightly, despite them. It is about standing firm in our principles when temptation or pressure tries to sway us. Courage empowers us to do what is right, even when no one is watching or when the stakes are high. It fuels our moral convictions, encouraging us to be honest, compassionate, and just. Without courage, moral values can become mere words. Sometimes, all it takes is a kind word, a sincere compliment, or a gentle reminder that we are capable of more than we realize. When others believe in us, it ignites a spark that pushes us to persevere through difficulties. When we ourselves encourage someone else, we help them discover their inner strength and resilience, inspiring personal growth and self-confidence. This mutual exchange of encouragement between people leaves a lasting impression. Moreover, encouragement nurtures the resilience necessary for moral development. It can be tempting to take shortcuts, to ignore injustice, or to act selfishly. In these moments, encouragement becomes vital. It reminds us that our actions matter and that choosing courage and integrity is always worth the effort. Encouragement reassures us that setbacks are temporary and that our moral character is something we can strengthen with perseverance and support. Remember, integrity advocates growth, and making conscious choices to grow better each day. Every act of kindness, every battle for truth, and every moment of integrity contributes to shaping our character. Encouragement helps us recognize these small victories and keeps us moving forward. It reminds us that even when we stumble, we have the power to get back up and continue on the path of goodness. To cultivate moral character through encouragement, we must also be willing to extend it to others. Genuine encouragement is rooted in sincerity and compassion. It requires us to see the potential in others, to celebrate their efforts, and to support them in their struggles. When we encourage others to be brave and true to themselves, we help foster a community of morally courageous individuals. This collective strength becomes a foundation upon which society can build equity, respect, and kindness.

Establishing a strong moral character is an essential foundation for leading a meaningful and fulfilling life. It is the process of creating and setting up a personal framework of values and principles that guide our decisions, actions, and interactions with others. Developing this moral backbone is not a one-time event but a lifelong journey that requires sincerity, reflection, and commitment.

At its core, establishing morals begins with self-awareness. It involves honestly examining who we are, what we believe in, and what kind of person we aspire to become. Take the time to reflect on your core values like honesty, kindness, integrity, respect, as well as compassion, and consider how these principles shape your perception of right and wrong. Recognizing what matters most to you is the first step in creating a moral compass that will serve as a guide in challenging situations.

Creating morals also involves learning from various sources such as family, community, culture, education, and personal experiences. These influences help shape your understanding of societal norms and ethical expectations. However, it is vital to approach this with sincerity and an open mind. Don't accept moral standards blindly. Instead, question and evaluate them critically, ensuring they align with your authentic beliefs, and contribute positively to your growth and the well-being of others.

Setting up morals is about more than just internal conviction. It's about actively committing to living by those principles. This means making conscious choices that reflect your values, even when it's difficult or inconvenient. For example, choosing honesty over deception, showing kindness in moments of frustration, or standing up for what is right despite opposition. These actions reinforce your moral character and help solidify your personal standards.

An essential aspect of establishing morals is consistency. Sincerity demands that we remain true to our principles across different situations and relationships. Being authentic in our moral commitments builds trust and respect from others, creating a foundation of integrity. It also fosters self-respect, as living in alignment with your values brings inner peace and confidence.

Furthermore, developing moral character involves ongoing education and self-improvement. Life presents numerous opportunities to practice virtues such as patience, humility, forgiveness, and empathy. By continuously striving to embody these qualities, you set up a moral character that is resilient and adaptable. Recognize that mistakes are part of the human experience. When you falter, sincere self-reflection and a willingness to learn from errors help you recalibrate and strengthen your morals.

Creating a moral character also extends to how you influence those around you. By setting up strong morals, you serve as a positive example for others, inspiring trust and fostering a community grounded in integrity and mutual respect. Your actions can motivate others to reflect on their own values and to establish their moral frameworks with sincerity. The world is constantly shifting and our values can be questioned, norms challenged, and societal expectations reshaped. The concept of having principles stands as a steadfast anchor amidst the tumult. Principles are the fundamental truths or beliefs that guide our behavior, shape our character, and influence our decisions. They are the moral compass that directs us toward integrity, authenticity, and purpose. To be principled with no limits is to hold unwavering beliefs that serve as a beacon of clarity and strength, regardless of circumstances or pressures. At their core, principles matter because they provide a foundation for tenacity and trust. When we operate based on clearly defined beliefs, others come to know what to expect from us. This predictability fosters trust in relationships whether personal, professional, or societal. Trust, after all, is built upon the expectation that individuals will act according to their values, even when it is inconvenient or challenging.

Moreover, principles serve as an internal moral compass. They help us navigate complex situations where the right course of action may not be immediately apparent. In moments of ambiguity, principles act as guiding stars, illuminating the path toward honesty, equity, compassion, and respect. They prevent us from being swayed by temporary temptations or external pressures that might lead us astray.

Having principles also cultivates resilience. When we are committed to core beliefs, setbacks and failures become opportunities for growth rather than excuses to abandon our values. Principles underpin perseverance, allowing us to stand firm in our convictions amidst adversity, criticism, or conflicting interests.

More importantly, principles matter because they influence the broader fabric of society. Societies founded on shared principles such as justice, equality, and freedom are more likely to thrive in harmony. When individuals uphold their principles, they contribute to a collective moral standard that sustains social cohesion and progression. To be principled with no limits means to hold one's core beliefs so deeply and sincerely that they transcend circumstances, temptations, or external influences. It signifies a commitment to live authentically and ethically, regardless of the cost or challenge. Such unwavering adherence is rooted in sincerity and a genuine desire to do what is right, not merely what is convenient or popular.

Living principled with no limits requires courage and humility. It demands that we stand by our values even when they are unpopular or when others may question our motives. It involves a willingness to accept personal sacrifice for the sake of integrity. It also necessitates a continuous reflection on our principles, ensuring they remain authentic and relevant, rather than dogmatic or rigid.

A principled life without limits is one characterized by consistency and a deep sense of purpose. It is about aligning our actions with our beliefs so thoroughly that there is harmony between what we say and what we do. This integrity engenders respect, not just from others, but within ourselves. It fosters a sense of inner peace, knowing that we are living according to our deepest convictions. Being sincere in one's principles means that they are not superficial or adopted for the sake of image. True principles are rooted in genuine care, empathy, and understanding of what is truly right. They are born out of reflection, experience, and a desire to contribute positively to the world. Sincerity ensures that principles are meaningful and enduring. When our beliefs are heartfelt, they guide us through the darkest nights and brightest days alike. They become part of our identity, shaping how we treat others and how we see ourselves.

Living principled with no limits is a noble pursuit that demands honesty, courage, perseverance, and humility. Principles matter because they uphold integrity, foster trust, guide us through complexity, and contribute to a just society. They are essential for personal growth and for building a world where equity and compassion prevail. In the end, principles are more than just rules. They are the expression of who we are and what we value most deeply. Honor is a cornerstone of human integrity and dignity. It is a principle that guides our actions, shapes our character, and defines how we are perceived by others. Why does honor matter? Honor is about staying true to oneself and maintaining a firm grasp of morality. It is the internal compass that aligns our actions with our values, ensuring that we act with honesty, equity, and compassion. When we prioritize honor, we foster trust and respect in our relationships, whether with family, friends, colleagues, or the community at large. This trust is the foundation upon which meaningful connections are built. Without it, relationships become fragile and superficial. Honoring oneself and others elevates our entire society. It encourages accountability and responsibility, urging us to stand by our commitments and admit our mistakes with humility. When individuals act honorably, it can cause others to follow suit. In this way, honor becomes a collective virtue, an essential ingredient for social harmony and progress. It cultivates an environment where justice prevails, and dignity is preserved for all. Furthermore, honor matters because it shapes our reputation and legacy. The way we conduct ourselves, especially in difficult times, leaves a lasting impression. True honor is not about fleeting recognition or superficial accolades, it is about the steadiness of good character that endures through life's trials. When we uphold our honor, we earn the respect of others and leave behind a legacy of integrity that can inspire future generations. Living honorably also brings personal fulfillment and inner peace. When our actions align with our values, we experience a profound sense of satisfaction and self-respect. Conversely, betraying our own sense of honor by acting dishonestly or selfishly leaves a mark of guilt and regret. Genuine honor requires courage and humility. It demands that we stand firm in our principles, even when faced with temptation or adversity. In addition, honor often involves sacrifice. It may mean choosing the right thing over the easy or popular choice. It may require humility to accept praise graciously or the strength to forgive those who have wronged us.

These acts reinforce our moral fiber and deepen our sense of purpose. They remind us that honor is not just about lofty ideals, but about everyday choices like small acts of kindness, honesty, or respect that collectively define who we are. Honor is not a mere abstract concept. It is a vital aspect of a meaningful life. It matters because it preserves our dignity, fosters trust, and shapes a just and compassionate society. Living honorably is a sincere commitment to embodying the virtues we hold dear like truth, respect, responsibility, and humility. In honoring ourselves and others, we contribute to a world where integrity prevails and human worth is truly valued. Let us cherish and uphold honor in all our endeavors, for through it, we forge a path toward a grander, more compassionate humanity. Among these virtues, decency stands out as a cornerstone of good character, an attribute that not only shapes our interactions with others but also enriches our inner lives. Being a decent person is more than just acting kindly or politely, it is a reflection of integrity, empathy, and respect that reverberates through every aspect of our existence. Decency is often seen as a fundamental moral quality, a standard of behavior that aligns with universal values of equity, kindness, honesty, and respect. It's about treating others with dignity, listening sincerely, and acting with genuine concern for their well-being. Decent people strive to do the right thing, end of story. They recognize the intrinsic worth of every individual, regardless of background, status, or circumstances. Being a decent person has its positives and negatives. Decent behavior cultivates trust. When we consistently treat others with respect and honesty, we build relationships rooted in reliability and mutual understanding. Friends, family, colleagues, and even strangers feel safe around us. Trust forms the foundation of deep connections, and such connections bring joy, support, and a sense of belonging, elements essential for our mental and emotional health. Decency is contagious. When we act kindly and ethically, we inspire others to do the same. Small acts of decency like offering a helping hand, listening without judgment, or showing gratitude can spark a chain reaction that elevates the moral fabric of our communities. Over time, these collective acts foster environments where kindness and respect can flourish. Living decently aligns with our core values and strengthens our sense of integrity. When our actions match our beliefs, we experience inner harmony and self-respect. Being decent cultivates a clear conscience, reduces internal conflict, and nurtures a sense of pride.

We can look at ourselves in the mirror and feel confident that we are living authentically. Decent individuals help create equitable, more compassionate communities. By acting justly and respectfully, we support social cohesion and work toward reducing conflicts and misunderstandings. Our collective decency can be a powerful force for societal progress, promoting inclusivity, justice, and peace.

Choosing to be decent often involves patience, humility, and self-awareness. These qualities push us to reflect on our actions and strive to improve. As we cultivate decency, we develop resilience and emotional intelligence. Such growth leads to a more satisfying life, filled with meaningful interactions and a sense of purpose. While fleeting pleasures can be tempting, lasting happiness often stems from meaningful relationships and contributing positively to others' lives. Decency fosters this lasting happiness because it builds genuine bonds and creates a sense of fulfillment that superficial gains cannot provide. Living decently nurtures a heart at peace and a mind free from guilt or regret. Choosing to be a decent person is an ongoing commitment. It requires mindfulness, patience, and a willingness to stand up for what is right, even when it's inconvenient. It's about making conscious choices, whether to forgive, to listen patiently, or to admit mistakes that align with our core values. In doing so, we not only improve ourselves but also influence the world around us. Being a decent person isn't always the easiest path, but it is undeniably one of the most rewarding. The benefits reaped from it like trust, strong relationships, personal integrity, societal harmony, and inner fulfillment are invaluable. In a time when cynicism and negativity often dominate, embodying decency reminds us of our shared humanity and the profound impact simple acts of kindness can have. Ultimately, decency nurtures a life of authenticity, connection, purpose, and having an existence that not only enriches ourselves but also makes the world a better place for everyone.

The concept of justice stands as a beacon of hope, an aspiration for equity and integrity. To speak of justice is to speak of a fundamental principle that guides us toward a society where every individual is valued, respected, and given the opportunity to succeed. It is not merely about the absence of wrongdoing but about fostering an environment where equity is woven into the very fabric of our interactions, policies, and systems.

At the heart of justice lies the principle of equity. Unlike equality, which might suggest treating everyone the same regardless of circumstances, equity recognizes that people's lives are shaped by different experiences, challenges, and opportunities. True justice demands that we acknowledge these differences and work intentionally to address disparities. It is about creating a level playing field, not by uniform treatment alone, but by providing the tailored support necessary for each person to succeed.

Equity requires us to listen deeply, to understand the barriers that prevent poverty stricken groups from accessing opportunities. It compels us to be honest about the ways historical injustices and systemic biases continue to influence present realities. For example, in education, equity means ensuring that students from underserved communities receive additional resources, mentorship, and support to bridge gaps that have been long-standing. In healthcare, it involves not just providing services but actively working to eliminate disparities rooted in socio-economic status, race, or geography.

To pursue justice with sincerity is to commit to ongoing reflection and humility. It asks us to confront our biases and privileges and to be willing to make sacrifices for the common good. It is about recognizing that equity is an active process that requires intentional effort, policy reform, and the cultivation of empathy. Genuine equity cannot be achieved through fake measures or lip service. It demands persistent action and a heartfelt dedication to change, real change.

Furthermore, justice grounded in equity recognizes the interconnectedness of all humanity. When one community suffers injustice, it diminishes us all. An equitable society is one where diversity is celebrated and where inclusion is not just a buzzword but a lived reality. It is about ensuring that everyone's voice is heard and that fringe of society groups are empowered to partake fully in societal life. Living with a sincere commitment to justice means holding ourselves accountable and challenging systems that perpetuate inequality. It involves advocating for policies that uplift the vulnerable and dismantle oppressive structures. It means fostering a culture of compassion where kindness and equity prevail over indifference or prejudice. See Case Law § **Isaiah 59:14**.

Ultimately, justice and equity are not a destination but an ongoing journey. It is a moral imperative that calls us to be better versions of ourselves and to strive relentlessly toward a world where equity is not an ideal but a tangible reality for all. When we embrace this path sincerely, driven by humility and a genuine desire to do right, we create a more just, compassionate, and equitable society that honors the dignity of every individual and reflects the best of our shared humanity. In the journey of life, one of the most profound realizations we can come to is that true power resides not solely within ourselves, but through divine guidance from Yahweh. Our minds are incredible gifts that are complex, capable, and filled with potential. Yet, without direction and understanding, that potential can remain dormant or even misused. It is in turning to Yahweh, the Creator of all, that we unlock the true power of our minds.

Yahweh is the Source of all wisdom and strength. When we seek His guidance, we acknowledge our limitations and recognize that we are not alone in our struggles, doubts, or uncertainties. The act of turning to Yahweh is an act of humility, a sincere acknowledgment that our own understanding is finite, and that divine insight is necessary for true enlightenment. See Case Law § **Proverbs 3:5-8** reminds us, "Trust in the LORD Yahweh with all thine heart; and lean not unto thine own understanding. 6. In all thy ways acknowledge him, and he shall direct thy paths. 7. Be not wise in thine own eyes: fear the LORD Yahweh, and depart from evil. 8. It shall be health to thy navel, and marrow to thy bones."

Our minds are powerful tools capable of creating, imagining, analyzing, and solving. However, their full potential can only be realized when aligned with divine wisdom. Prayer, meditation, and scripture study serve as channels for us to connect with Yahweh's guidance. Through these spiritual practices, we invite His Spirit to dwell within us, illuminating our thoughts and empowering us to think clearly, compassionately, and rightly. When we do this, we begin to see that our thoughts and intentions are not isolated phenomena but are connected to a divine purpose.

Turning to Yahweh also involves trust and patience. Often, the answers we seek or the clarity we desire may not come immediately. Yet, by consistently seeking His guidance, we develop a deeper understanding that His timing and His plan are perfect. This ongoing reliance builds a foundation of faith, strengthening our mental resilience and inner peace. It is in this surrendered state that our minds become a conduit for divine power rather than a source of confusion or chaos. Moreover, Yahweh's power within us can transform our thoughts and attitudes. When we consciously seek His presence and wisdom, our minds are renewed and our perspectives are expanded. We begin to see opportunities instead of obstacles, hope instead of despair, and love instead of fear. This mental shift is evidence of Yahweh's power actively working within us, guiding our thoughts, shaping our beliefs, and inspiring us to act in ways that reflect His goodness. The sincerity of our heart in seeking Yahweh's guidance is paramount. It's not merely a ritual or a fleeting moment of prayer, but a genuine desire to align our entire being with His will. In doing so, we tap into the divine power that Yahweh grants to His followers.

This power is not forceful or manipulative but gentle, transformative, and enduring. It empowers us to overcome challenges, to forgive, to serve others, and to pursue truth with unwavering conviction. See Case Law § **Psalms 18:32**.

In essence, the power of the mind is a sacred gift from Yahweh and an opportunity for us to participate in His divine plan. When we turn to Him wholeheartedly, with sincerity and humility, He grants us His strength, clarity, and wisdom. Our thoughts become tools for good, our decisions grounded in divine truth, and our lives a reflection of His glory. Let us, therefore, continually seek Yahweh's guidance, trusting that His power within us is greater than any obstacle we face. Through sincere devotion and reliance on Him, we unlock the full potential of our minds and walk in the power and purpose that He so graciously provides. Honesty is a virtue that lies at the very heart of our existence, a quality that transcends culture, language, and time. In a world often filled with deception, half-truths, and dishonesty, the call for genuine integrity grows louder and more urgent. As followers of Yahweh, we are called to a higher standard to live with honesty in every aspect of our lives. Yahweh desires us to be honest because honesty reflects His own nature which is pure, truthful, and just. It is through our honesty that we can truly mirror His character and bring light into a darkened world.

The world today is desperately in need of honest souls. Everywhere we look, we see signs of betrayal and insincerity like in politics, business, personal relationships, and even within ourselves. People are craving truth, authenticity, and integrity. They long for someone who will speak honestly, act sincerely, and live transparently. When honest individuals stand firm amidst a sea of dishonesty, they become beacons of hope. Their lives demonstrate that integrity is possible, that truth still matters, and that a life built on honesty is a life worth living. Yahweh's desire for honesty is rooted in His steadfast love and justice. He knows that honesty cultivates trust — trust in Him, in others, and within ourselves. When we are honest, we create a foundation of reliability and credibility. People can count on us not just because we say the right things, but because our actions align with our words. This consistency nurtures relationships, strengthens communities, and fosters a culture of respect and just measures. In a world where falsehoods can easily spread and where deception can seem advantageous, living honestly is an act of courage and faith. Moreover, honesty is not always easy. It requires humility to admit our faults, bravery to speak the truth even when it's uncomfortable, and perseverance to stay committed to integrity in the face of temptation or pressure. But Yahweh promises that such honesty will lead to a fulfilled life characterized by peace, inner wholeness, and divine favor. He understands that honesty is a reflection of our love for Him and our respect for others. When we choose honesty, we honor His commandments and demonstrate our trust in His divine providence. The importance of honesty extends beyond individual conduct. It impacts society as a whole. A community that values honesty becomes a safe place where trust and cooperation flourish. It is a community where justice prevails, and people are not ruled by suspicion or fear but by mutual respect and truth. As believers, we are called to lead by example, to be honest in our dealings, and to advocate for truth in every sphere of life. Our honesty can inspire others to live authentically and to seek the truth, thereby transforming communities and nations for good. In our journey of faith, honesty also deepens our relationship with Yahweh. It requires us to be honest about our shortcomings, our doubts, and our struggles. When we come before Him with sincerity, Yahweh meets us with mercy and compassion.

Our honesty becomes a form of worship and an acknowledgment that we need His guidance and forgiveness. Through honesty, we open ourselves to His transforming power, allowing us to become more like Yahweh, who embodied perfect truth and integrity. Ultimately, Yahweh's desire is for us to be honest not merely because it's a moral obligation, but because honesty is a reflection of His divine character. When we choose truth and integrity, we participate in His divine plan for a just and righteous world. We become witnesses to His truth and carriers of His light. The world needs honest souls now more than ever; People who stand firm in truth, who speak with sincerity, and who live with integrity. In doing so, we fulfill His desire for us and contribute to a world that longs for honesty and justice. Let us then commit ourselves anew to living honestly, trusting that in our sincerity, we honor Yahweh and serve as His witnesses. May our lives be a testament to His truth, inspiring others to embrace honesty and to build a world where integrity reigns. For in honesty, we find not only our purpose but also the reflection of Yahweh's divine love shining through us. Now on to ethics, the reflection of Yahweh's desire for us to do good. In our journey through life, one of the most profound pursuits we can undertake is the knowledge of ethics, the principles and values that guide our actions and shape our character. At the very heart of this pursuit lies a divine truth: Yahweh, the Creator of all, desires us to embody ethical behavior. Ethics is not merely a set of rules to follow. It is a reflection of our respect for the divine order, our love for others, and our commitment to living rightly. Yahweh's call for ethical living is rooted in His nature. He is just, merciful, and loving. Throughout the scriptures, we see that He cares deeply about how we treat one another. From the commandment to love our neighbors as ourselves, to the call to justice and mercy, the Divine design emphasizes the importance of ethics, putting principles into practice in our daily lives. This work is ongoing, requiring sincerity, humility, and a willingness to align our actions with divine standards. Ethics work is not always easy. It challenges us to examine our motives, confront our biases, and make difficult choices. When we commit ourselves to ethical conduct, we honor Yahweh's intention for us to be responsible stewards of His creation and compassionate members of society. Living ethically also involves active engagement. It's about actively doing good.

This means standing up for justice, helping those in need, speaking out against injustice, and being honest in our dealings. Such work requires sincerity and an authentic desire to reflect divine goodness in our actions. It's a continuous effort to promote virtues like kindness, patience, humility, and equity. Furthermore, ethics work is deeply relational. It influences how we interact with others, shaping communities founded on trust, respect, and love. When we practice ethics, we not only obey divine commandments but also contribute to healing and building up our neighborhoods and nations. Our ethical commitments serve as a testament to our faith and our understanding that Yahweh's commandments are meant to bring about peace and well-being for all. It's important to recognize that ethical living is a journey, not a destination. We will inevitably stumble and fall short at times, but Yahweh's grace is always available to restore and renew us. The sincerity of our desire to do right matters more than perfection. As we strive to align our lives with divine principles, we deepen our relationship with Yahweh and become more effective agents of His love and justice. In conclusion, ethics are a vital expression of Yahweh's will for us. It embodies our commitment to living right, caring genuinely for others, and upholding the divine order. As we embrace this calling, we participate in the divine mission to bring light and hope into a world that desperately needs it. Let us pursue ethical living with humility and sincerity, trusting that through our efforts, we honor Yahweh and contribute to His kingdom of righteousness on earth. Establishing moral character is a deliberate act of creating and setting up a personal code of ethics rooted in sincerity and genuine conviction. It requires introspection, critical evaluation of influences, consistent practice, and the courage to uphold principles even in adversity. As you build this moral foundation, you not only shape your own life but also contribute to a more honest, compassionate, and just society. Remember, the journey to moral integrity is ongoing, and each step taken with sincerity brings you closer to becoming the person you aspire to be. Encouragement and courage are intertwined in the great pursuit of moral character. They serve as the guiding light that leads us through life's complexities and challenges. By encouraging ourselves and others to act with integrity and bravery, we nurture a moral spirit that is resilient and enduring.

Let us remember that each kind word, each act of support, and each moment of courage, no matter how small, is a vital step towards becoming better, more upright human beings. Together, through encouragement and courage, we can build a world rooted in moral strength, compassion, and hope. Being upright encompasses more than just posture or outward appearance. It is a sincere reflection of one's moral character and a commitment to living honestly and ethically. Whether physical or moral, uprightness signifies alignment whether with the truth, justice, or one's principles, that fosters trust, respect, and dignity. Embracing uprightness is a lifelong journey of self-awareness, morality, and courage. It ultimately shapes a life of integrity and respect, inspiring others to follow suit.

Chapter 2

Living a righteous life is a noble aspiration that many of us hold deep within our hearts. It's a journey of continuous growth, self-awareness, and genuine intention. Righteousness is about striving to be good, honest, and just in every aspect of our lives. If you truly wish to be righteous, it begins with setting a clear goal and committing yourself to that path with sincerity and humility. The first and most vital step toward righteousness is defining what being good means to you. Without a clear goal, it's easy to drift or become complacent. Take time to reflect on your values, principles, and the kind of person you want to be. Do you want to be honest, compassionate, generous, or just? Or perhaps a combination of these qualities? Write down your aspirations and keep them in mind as a guiding light. Having a concrete goal helps you stay focused and motivated. It's like setting a destination on a journey. You need to know where you're headed to navigate effectively. Remember, righteousness is a lifelong pursuit. To be righteous, you must first understand yourself. Be honest about your strengths and weaknesses, your motives, and your behaviors. Self-awareness allows you to recognize where you fall short and helps you to make conscious adjustments. Regular reflection, meditation, or journaling can help deepen your understanding of yourself. Honesty is the foundation of righteousness. Always speak the truth, even when it's difficult. Avoid deceit or manipulation, and be sincere in your dealings with others. Authenticity creates trust and respect, which are essential for a righteous life. Cultivate compassion and kindness in your daily interactions. Show empathy to those around you by trying to listen attentively, understand their perspectives, and offer help when needed. Acts of kindness, no matter how small, reinforce your commitment to goodness.

Whether it's a kind word, a helping hand, or forgiving someone who wronged you, these actions promote harmony and reflect your inner righteousness. Being righteous involves standing up for what is right, even when it's inconvenient or unpopular. Be open-minded and just in your decisions, and advocate for those who are oppressed or marginalized. Avoid favoritism or prejudice. Strive to create equity in your community and relationships. Justice requires courage and integrity. Sometimes, it means speaking out against injustice or making difficult choices. Remember, righteousness isn't passive, it's active and intentional. No one is perfect, and everyone makes mistakes. Embrace humility and see errors as opportunities to learn and grow. When you stumble, acknowledge your faults, seek forgiveness if needed, and commit to doing better. Stay open to new insights, be willing to admit when you're wrong, and remain humble in your pursuit of goodness. Consistency is key to righteousness. Strive to embody your principles in every aspect of your life such as at work, at home, in your community, and within yourself. Small acts of integrity accumulate over time, shaping your character and reputation. When you face temptations or challenges, remember your goal to be good. Use your values as a compass to guide your decisions. Surround yourself with righteous influences whether it be wise friends, mentors, spiritual guides, or inspiring literature. Learning from others' experiences and insights can strengthen your resolve and broaden your understanding of righteousness. Also, don't hesitate to seek support during difficult times. Righteous living is not about doing everything alone. Community and shared values can uplift you and keep you on the right path. Becoming truly righteous takes time and effort. There will be setbacks and days when you feel discouraged. Practice patience and remind yourself that every small step toward goodness counts. Perseverance is vital. Keep renewing your commitment, learn from your mistakes, and celebrate your progress. Over time, your character will become more aligned with your ideals. Being righteous is a heartfelt journey rooted in sincere effort and unwavering commitment. It begins with setting a clear goal to be good, understanding yourself honestly, and living with compassion, justice, humility, and perseverance. By approaching this path with sincerity and patience, you will find fulfillment not only in your own growth but also in the positive impact you have on others.

Stay true to your values, keep your heart open, and walk steadily toward righteousness. Understanding how to earn respect in Yahweh's eyes is a profound journey that calls for sincerity, humility, and a genuine desire to live according to His divine principles. Respect in the eyes of Yahweh is not merely about outward appearances or superficial actions, it is about cultivating a heart that aligns with His righteousness and demonstrates unwavering faith and love. If you seek to be truly respectable before Yahweh, consider the following principles that guide a life pleasing in His sight. The foundation of earning respect in Yahweh's eyes begins with reverence. Proverbs 1:7 tells us that, "The fear of Yahweh is the beginning of knowledge." This fear is not about being afraid but about honoring Yahweh's holiness, sovereignty, and justice. When you recognize His greatness and submit to His authority, you demonstrate a respectful attitude that He values deeply. It involves acknowledging His power, trusting His plans, and living with humility before Him. Yahweh values sincerity over superficial religious acts. See Case Law **§ Matthew 15:8-9** "This people draweth nigh unto me with their mouth, and honoureth me with *their* lips; but their heart is far from me. 9 But in vain they do worship me, teaching *for* doctrines the commandments of men." To earn His respect, your worship, prayers, and acts of service must come from genuine love and devotion. Avoid hypocrisy or performing religious duties simply out of obligation. Instead, let your actions reflect a sincere desire to please Yahweh and follow His commandments. Obedience is a key aspect of earning respect in Yahweh's eyes. See Case Law **§ Deuteronomy 10:12-13** urges us, "And now, Israel, what doth the LORD Yahweh thy God require of thee, but to fear the LORD Yahweh thy God, to walk in all his ways, and to love him, and to serve the LORD Yahweh thy God with all thy heart and with all thy soul, 13. To keep the commandments of the LORD Yahweh, and his statutes, which I command thee this day for thy good." Living a life of obedience is a demonstration of trust and respect for His divine laws. When you follow His commandments not out of fear of punishment but out of love and reverence, you show that you honor His authority and desire to walk in righteousness. No one is perfect though we should work towards it, and acknowledging your imperfections is vital in earning Yahweh's respect.

See Case Law § **Psalm 51:17** says, "The sacrifices of Yahweh are a broken spirit; a broken and contrite heart, O Yahweh, you will not despise." Genuine humility and readiness to repent when you falter shows integrity and a sincere heart. Yahweh respects those who recognize their dependence on Him and seek His forgiveness and guidance. Respect in Yahweh's eyes is also reflected in how you treat others. See Case Law § **Proverbs 11:3** states, "The integrity of the upright shall guide them: but the perverseness of transgressors shall destroy them." Conducting yourself with honesty, equity, and kindness demonstrates that you value His teachings on justice and love. When your actions reflect His moral standards, you earn His respect and become a witness of His righteousness. Yahweh is a God of compassion and love. As His follower, embody these virtues in your daily life. See Case Law § **Matthew 22:37-39** emphasizes loving Yahweh with all your heart and loving your neighbor as yourself. Showing genuine concern, kindness, and patience towards others mirrors Yahweh's character and aligns your life with His expectations. Such qualities earn His admiration because they reflect His nature. Respect in Yahweh's eyes involves a humble acknowledgment that spiritual growth is ongoing. See Case Law § **Psalm 119:105** describes Yahweh's word as a "NUN. Thy word *is* a lamp unto my feet, and a light unto my path." Regularly studying His Word, praying earnestly, and seeking His guidance show your commitment to grow closer to Him. When you prioritize spiritual development, you demonstrate respect for His wisdom and authority. Earning respect in Yahweh's eyes is a lifelong pursuit rooted in sincerity, humility, obedience, integrity, and love. It begins with reverence for His holiness and extends into every aspect of your life like how you treat others, how you conduct yourself, and how you seek to grow spiritually. Remember, Yahweh is a God who values the heart above all else. By aligning your heart with His divine will, living authentically, and showing genuine love and humility, you will earn His respect and draw closer to the divine grace that He freely offers. Strive daily to reflect His character, and in doing so, you will find yourself more in harmony with His divine purpose for your life. When we stay true to Yahweh's moral attributes, we express approval of goodness and integrity, and disapproval of dishonesty, injustice, or harm. Involving ourselves morally means more than passive judgment.

It is an active choice to live with authenticity and responsibility. Every decision we make, from small daily acts to significant life choices, reflects our commitment to doing what is right. When faced with dilemmas or temptations, we must ask ourselves what integrity demands of us. In doing so, we involve our whole selves (mind, heart, and conscience) in the pursuit of moral clarity. Our actions become expressions of moral approval when they align with principles of equity, kindness, and honesty. Our actions can also become expressions of moral disapproval when they violate these principles. Staying true requires morality and courage. It involves resisting societal pressures, peer influence, or personal shortcuts that compromise our integrity. At times, this may mean speaking out against injustice, confronting uncomfortable truths, or making sacrifices that others might not understand. It is in these moments that our true character is revealed, and our commitment to doing what is right becomes evident. Moreover, staying true fosters trust and respect both from ourselves and from others. When we consistently act in accordance with our moral convictions, we reinforce our integrity and credibility. People recognize authenticity and are often inspired by those who remain steadfast in their principles. Conversely, disapproval of dishonesty or betrayal reveals a recognition of the importance of moral standards and the need to uphold them for the collective good. Ultimately, doing what is right is not always about perfection; it is about persistence and humility. It involves acknowledging our imperfections and striving to grow in virtue. Staying true is a lifelong journey and a continual effort to align our actions with our deepest moral convictions. It calls us to reflect regularly on our choices, to learn from our mistakes, and to recommit to the values that define us. In a broader sense, staying true is a moral act that contributes to a more just, compassionate, and authentic world. When individuals choose to act with integrity, they ripple out positive change that can inspire others to do the same. It is a collective effort. Each person's commitment to doing what is right helps to build communities rooted in trust, respect, and moral responsibility. Stay true to Yahweh. Let your actions be a testament to your moral convictions. Involving yourself morally and expressing disapproval of injustice when necessary, you participate in the ongoing pursuit of what is right. Remember, true integrity is not just about adhering to principles when it's easy, but about standing firm in your morals through every challenge and temptation.

In doing so, you honor your own dignity and contribute to a world where goodness and truth prevail. The world is filled with complexities, distractions, and often conflicting signals about what is right or wrong. It becomes vital to anchor ourselves in the pursuit of integrity and honesty. At the core of this pursuit lies the concept of being "straight", not just in our actions, but in the very fabric of our minds and hearts. For Yahweh, the Creator of all, a straight and honest mind is not merely a virtue but a divine expectation. He desires us to cultivate a heart that is sincere, upright, and aligned with His truth.

Throughout Scripture, Yahweh emphasizes the importance of having a right or honest mind. See Case Law **§ Proverbs 3:5-6**, we are encouraged to trust in Yahweh with all our heart and to lean not on our own understanding, but to acknowledge Him in all our ways, and He will make our paths straight. This "straight" path signifies a life guided by divine wisdom, integrity, and uprightness. Yahweh wants us to think honestly, to evaluate our motives critically, and to pursue righteousness in all our dealings. A right-minded person is one who seeks truth sincerely, who recognizes that honesty begins within the mind. It is not enough to outwardly conform or to pretend righteousness. Yahweh looks at the heart, motives, and thoughts that drive our actions. A straight mind is free from deception, selfishness, and cruelty. It is rooted in humility, transparency, and a genuine desire to do what is right before Him and others. Being "straight" in our thinking means more than just avoiding overt wrongdoings. It involves cultivating honesty within our inner dialogue. Our thoughts shape our words, our actions, and ultimately our character. When our minds are honest and aligned with Yahweh's truth, our lives reflect that integrity. This alignment helps us navigate life's challenges with clarity and moral courage. For instance, when faced with a difficult decision, a straight-minded person seeks Yahweh's guidance, praying for wisdom and discernment. They evaluate their motives honestly and consider how their choices affect others. Such individuals hold themselves accountable, recognizing that true righteousness begins with honest assessment of oneself. Honesty is the foundation of a straight heart. Yahweh calls us to be truthful in our speech and genuine in our intentions.

See Case Law **§ Proverbs 12:22** states, "Lying lips *are* abomination to the LORD Yahweh: but they that deal truly *are* his delight." This highlights that Yahweh values honesty deeply. To be right-minded means to consistently choose truth over deception, integrity over compromise. Uprightness or righteousness also involves aligning our actions with Yahweh's commandments. It requires consistency with our thoughts, words, and deeds working together in harmony. When we maintain a straight mind, we are less likely to be swayed by temptation or peer pressure. Instead, we stand firm on Yahweh's principles, striving to live in a way that pleases Him. Living with a straight and honest mind is an act of faith. It reflects trust in Yahweh's goodness and His desire for our well-being. It is a daily choice to reject deceit and to pursue truth, even when it is difficult or inconvenient. Such a life demonstrates our love for Yahweh and our respect for His creation. This commitment to honesty and integrity also influences our relationships. When others see us as truthful and upright, they are more likely to trust us and see the character of Yahweh reflected in our lives. Our sincerity can serve as a testimony that leads others toward the truth and the righteousness found in Yahweh. Yahweh understands that a truly straight and honest mind does not develop overnight. It is the result of continual surrender, prayer, study of His Word, and deliberate effort. He promises to help us in this journey, transforming our hearts and renewing our minds (see Case Law **§ Romans 12:2**). When we seek Him earnestly, He grants us wisdom and a desire to live rightly. Ultimately, being right-minded is about aligning ourselves with Yahweh's way, allowing His truth to shape our thoughts and actions. It involves humility, self-awareness, and a sincere commitment to walk in righteousness. As we pursue this path, we become living testimonies of His grace, reflecting the straightness of His character and drawing others into His light. Yahweh wants us to have a right or honest mind not just for our own sake, but because such a life honors Him and exemplifies His righteousness. Living straight begins within the heart and mind and extends outward in our words and deeds. It is a daily pursuit, a spiritual discipline rooted in trust, humility, and love.

May we continually seek Yahweh's guidance to cultivate a sincere, honest, and straight mind. In doing so, we align ourselves with His divine purpose, walking the path of righteousness that leads to life, joy, and true fulfillment in Him. When considering what it means to be truly "fit," whether from a moral, social, or personal standpoint, one must recognize that the concept extends far beyond mere physical appearance or superficial assessments. At its core, being fit encompasses the qualities of being seemingly and proper, not only in body but also in character and demeanor. It is about aligning oneself with the standards of decency, appropriateness, and respect that uphold the integrity of our interactions and societal expectations.

From a moral perspective, being fit involves cultivating virtues such as humility, kindness, and honesty. These qualities ensure that one's actions and words are seemingly in the eyes of others, fostering trust and mutual respect. When a person demonstrates moral fitness, they act in ways that are proper and appropriate, considering the well-being of those around them. Such conduct reflects an internal harmony that makes one seem trustworthy and genuinely upright in character. Morally fit individuals embody integrity, ensuring their behavior aligns with ethical principles, thereby earning the respect of their community. In social contexts, being seemingly and proper is equally vital. It involves understanding the nuances of social etiquette, displaying good manners, and respecting cultural norms. To be socially fit means being aware of the appropriate way to conduct oneself in various situations whether in formal gatherings, casual conversations, or professional environments. This awareness not only ensures one's actions are seemingly but also demonstrates a sincere regard for others' comfort and dignity. When someone is socially fit, they are perceived as considerate, well-mannered, and suitable for their roles within different social settings. Such qualities contribute to harmonious relationships and uphold the decorum that keeps society functioning smoothly. On a personal level, being fit also entails a genuine commitment to self-improvement and self-awareness. It means dressing appropriately for the occasion, which is a tangible way of showing respect for oneself and others.

Proper attire and grooming are not merely superficial concerns, but are expressions of a person's understanding of appropriateness and their desire to present themselves in a seemingly manner. When one takes care to be properly dressed and well-groomed, it communicates sincerity and respect. It is an acknowledgment that their appearance should reflect their inner values and the context they are in. Furthermore, moral and social fitness involve embodying qualities that make one seem proper in their interactions. This includes listening attentively, speaking thoughtfully, and acting with compassion. Such behaviors are essential to maintaining decorum and ensuring relationships are built on mutual respect. When a person consistently exhibits these virtues, they are seen as genuinely fitting, someone whose presence and conduct are appropriate, sincere, and contribute positively to their environment.

It is important to recognize that being seemingly and proper is not about superficial perfection but about authenticity and intention. True fitness in this sense is rooted in sincerity, living in a manner that aligns with one's values and the expectations of goodness and respect. It is about understanding what is fitting in each moment, adapting with humility, and striving to embody qualities that elevate oneself and those around them.

To be acceptable from the standpoint of competence or morality involves more than just outward appearances. It requires a sincere effort to be seemingly and proper in all facets of life. Whether through moral virtues, social awareness, or personal presentation, genuine fitness lies in embodying qualities that uphold integrity, respect, and decency. When we strive for this kind of fitness, we foster trust and harmony in our communities, ensuring that our actions and demeanor reflect the best of who we are and what we value. In the quiet moments of reflection, when the world slows down and our hearts turn inward, there emerges a profound truth: Our purpose is rooted in service. To serve Yahweh is to align ourselves with the Divine will and to dedicate our lives to something greater than ourselves. It is the highest calling, a sacred invitation to be of genuine value to the Creator who lovingly crafted us.

Serving Yahweh is about embodying a sincere desire to be of use in His divine plan. It is an act of humility, recognizing that our existence has meaning only when we are willing to contribute to His purpose. When we serve with sincerity, we acknowledge that every breath, every act of kindness, every moment of patience is an offering to our Lord Yahweh. It transforms everyday normal moments into moments of worship and devotion.

To be of use to Yahweh requires a heartfelt commitment. It means seeking to reflect His love, mercy, and justice in our words and deeds. It involves listening carefully to His guidance through prayer, Scripture, and the quiet whisperings of conscience. It requires patience and persistence, understanding that service is often a steady, unrecognized labor like the gentle tending of a garden, or the silent support of a loved one that ultimately bears fruit in the divine timing.

Serving Yahweh also entails recognizing the sacredness of others. When we serve our neighbors, our friends, and even strangers, we participate in His divine work. Every act of kindness, every moment of compassion, becomes a tangible expression of our devotion. In serving others, we serve Yahweh Himself, for He is present in each person, each creature, and each act of goodness. To be of use, then, is to extend love and help to those in need, knowing that in doing so, we are fulfilling His command to love one another.

A sincere servant of Yahweh understands that service is not always glamorous or easy. It often requires sacrifice, patience, and humility. Yet, in these acts of selflessness, we find true fulfillment and peace. Our service is a response to His love, an acknowledgment that we are His workers, His instruments of grace and mercy in this world. When we serve with a genuine heart, we become a living testimony of His goodness and faithfulness.

Furthermore, serving Yahweh is a lifelong journey. It involves continuous growth, learning, and surrender. It calls us to examine our motives and to ensure that our service is rooted in sincerity rather than obligation or pride. A true servant understands that their worth is not measured by recognition or accolades but by the faithfulness of their heart's intent.

In committing to serve Yahweh, we also find purpose and direction amid life's uncertainties. Our service becomes a compass that guides our choices and actions. It reminds us that our lives are not our own but are entrusted to us by a loving Father who desires us to be active participants in His divine plan. Our acts of service, no matter how small they seem, ripple outward, touching lives and advancing His kingdom here on earth.

Ultimately, to serve Yahweh is to live in love and humility, to be of use in His divine design. It is a sincere act of devotion that transforms us from mere individuals into vessels of His grace. When we serve with sincerity, we honor our Creator, bring hope to others, and find deep fulfillment in our purpose. Let us embrace this calling wholeheartedly, knowing that in serving Yahweh, we truly become our best selves (servants of love, truth, and everlasting life).

Virtue is often spoken of as an ideal or an aspirational quality that guides our actions and shapes our character. It is the pursuit of moral excellence, the commitment to doing what is right in the eyes of Yahweh. At its core, virtue is about integrity, compassion, humility, patience, and an unwavering dedication to the good. It is a lifelong journey, one that calls us to continually reflect, improve, and act with sincerity and purpose. One of the most essential aspects of virtue is efficacy, which is the ability to effect positive change through our actions. Efficacy in this context is not merely about achieving superficial results or gaining recognition, it is about making a meaningful difference in the lives of others and in the world around us. When we strive to be efficacious in our virtue, we recognize that real moral goodness is active, not passive. It demands effort and intentionality. It requires us to move beyond mere intentions and hopes to tangible deeds that uplift, support, and nurture. Being efficacious in virtue means understanding that our actions, no matter how small, can ripple outward and influence the larger fabric of society. It is about translating our moral principles into concrete acts such as helping a neighbor in need, speaking out against injustice, showing kindness in moments of frustration, and persevering in the face of challenges.

Virtue is not a static quality. It is a dynamic force that grows stronger when put into practice. To be efficacious is to recognize that our moral commitments are not just ideals to admire, but callings to fulfill. Sincerity is the foundation upon which true virtue is built. When our efforts are genuine, our actions carry authentic power. Sincere virtue resonates because it springs from the core of our being, reflecting our true values and intentions. This sincerity fosters trust and credibility, inspiring others to pursue their own virtuous paths. It also sustains us through difficult times, reminding us that our efforts are rooted in integrity and a genuine desire to do good. Living with virtue requires humility, an acknowledgment that we are imperfect and that our journey toward moral excellence is ongoing. Efficacy does not mean perfection, it means perseverance and a willingness to learn from our mistakes.

When we act sincerely, we are open to feedback, aware of our limitations, and committed to continual growth. This humility keeps us grounded and prevents us from becoming self-righteous or complacent. It reminds us that virtue is a lifelong pursuit, not a destination to be reached overnight.

Furthermore, being efficacious in virtue involves cultivating patience and resilience. Change often takes time, and the fruits of our good deeds may not be immediately visible. Yet, persistence matters. Each act of kindness, each moment of integrity, contributes to a larger ripple effect that can influence hearts and minds beyond our immediate sight. True efficacy recognizes that lasting goodness is often slow and steady, requiring dedication and unwavering faith in the possibility of making a difference. The pursuit of virtue also demands courage. Being efficacious and virtuous is powerful because both are rooted in a sincere conviction that doing good is worth the effort, regardless of the obstacles. This courage inspires others and creates a culture of moral strength that can uplift communities and foster lasting change. Ultimately, virtue is about becoming a better person, not for recognition or reward, but because it is the right thing to do. It is about aligning our values with our actions, ensuring that sincerity guides our efforts and efficacy amplifies their impact.

When we live with virtue, we become agents of positive change, not only improving ourselves but also enriching those around us. Our lives gain meaning and purpose when lived with the intention of embodying goodness in a genuine, efficacious manner. Virtue is a noble endeavor that calls us to be effective in our moral efforts and sincere in our intentions. It invites us to act with integrity, to persist through challenges, and to recognize that even small, sincere acts can have profound effects. By embracing virtue in all aspects of life, we contribute to a more compassionate, just, and humane world with one act of goodness at a time. Let us strive not only to be virtuous in our ideals but also efficacious in our deeds, living out the truth that genuine virtue transforms lives and makes the world a better place. When it comes to making choices in life, we are often faced with a multitude of options. Some are tempting, some are convenient, and others may seem appealing at first glance. Yet, amid all these choices, there is a profound truth that guides those who seek to live rightly: Yahweh, our Creator, only accepts what is of the best. This principle is not merely about preference or standards but about aligning our hearts and actions with what is truly good, pure, and worthy in His sight.

Yahweh, in His infinite wisdom and holiness, does not settle for less. He looks beyond the surface and examines the heart's motives, the quality of our offerings, and the integrity of our choices. When He asks for sacrifices or offerings, He desires the best, nothing marred or tainted, nothing less than what is excellent. This is a reflection of His own perfection and purity. If we are to be His people, then our choices must mirror this standard. We must only like and accept things that are of good quality, that are genuine, and that honor Him.

Choosing the best is a matter of sincerity. It is about giving our genuine best, not just what is easy or what requires the least effort. When we select our words, our actions, our possessions, or our relationships, we should ask ourselves if our choice reflects the excellence that Yahweh expects. Is it faithful, honest, pure, and true? Because if we acknowledge and observe only the things of good quality, we demonstrate our respect for Yahweh's standards and our desire to please Him.

Furthermore, the concept of choosing only what is good quality extends beyond material possessions; It influences our attitudes, our integrity, and our character. It challenges us to reject mediocrity and compromise. It calls us to seek excellence in our work, kindness in our interactions, and purity in our hearts. When we are intentional in this way, our lives become a testament to our devotion and our recognition that Yahweh deserves the very best.

This principle also encourages patience and discernment. Not everything that glitters is gold. Not every quick solution or cheap shortcut is of good quality. We must be willing to wait and seek what is truly valuable and enduring. In doing so, we cultivate a spirit of discernment, ensuring our choices are rooted in wisdom and integrity. It's a loving act to choose only what is good and acceptable to Yahweh because it reflects our respect for His holiness and our desire to honor Him with our lives.

The heart of this message is clear: We should like only those things that are of good quality such as things that are pure, genuine, and worthy of our Creator. Yahweh only accepts the best because He is the best. As His children, our goal should be to mirror His excellence in all our choices. Let us strive daily to select what is of true worth, to offer Him our best, and to live in a way that pleases and honors Him. In doing so, we align ourselves with His divine standards, and our lives become a pleasing aroma to Him, a reflection of His goodness and perfection. In our journey through life, we are often faced with choices, circumstances, and individuals that require us to exercise discernment, which is the ability to distinguish what is true from what is false, what is right from what is wrong, and what is beneficial from what is harmful. Discernment is a gift that enables us to navigate the complexities of human existence with wisdom and clarity. Yet, in contemplating the nature of discernment, it is vital to acknowledge the profound distinction between human judgment and divine discrimination, particularly in the context of Yahweh, the Creator and sustainer of all things.

Yahweh, as described throughout the scriptures, is not a passive observer but an active participant in the moral and spiritual affairs of the world. One of the most striking aspects of His divine nature is His ability to discriminate as well as His capacity to distinguish between individuals, nations, and choices based on righteousness, justice, and holiness. This discrimination is not arbitrary or biased but rooted in perfect wisdom and unwavering justice. It is an essential aspect of His divine character, reflecting His holiness and His commitment to uphold righteousness. The scriptures reveal numerous instances where Yahweh discriminates, not out of favoritism or prejudice, but as an expression of His justice. For example, in the story of Noah, Yahweh distinguishes between the righteous and the wicked, choosing to preserve a remnant of the faithful while condemning the corrupt generation. Similarly, in the story of Egypt and Israel, Yahweh discriminates by favoring His chosen people, delivering them from oppression while judging their oppressors. These acts of divine discrimination serve a higher purpose. They uphold divine justice and affirm the moral order of creation.

It is crucial to understand that Yahweh's discrimination is different from human prejudice. Humans often discriminate based on superficial factors such as race, ethnicity, social status, or personal bias. Such discrimination can be unjust, harmful, and rooted in ignorance. In contrast, Yahweh's discrimination is always righteous because it is based on His perfect knowledge and moral standards. His judgments are aligned with truth and justice, and His decisions are motivated by love, holiness, and the desire to bring about righteousness. Furthermore, Yahweh's discrimination offers a model for human discernment. As followers of Him, we are called to imitate His justice and mercy. Discernment, in the divine sense, involves recognizing the moral truth and aligning ourselves with what is good and true. It also involves rejecting prejudice and partiality, understanding that divine discernment is rooted in righteousness rather than favoritism. We are challenged to develop our own ability to discern between what is beneficial and harmful, or what leads to salvation and what leads to damnation, while also acknowledging that our judgments are limited and imperfect compared to divine wisdom.

Recognizing Yahweh's discrimination also calls us to humility. We must accept that our understanding is finite and that Divine judgment surpasses human comprehension. There are aspects of divine discrimination that we may not fully grasp, but we can trust in His perfect justice and goodness. This trust encourages us to seek divine guidance in our decisions and to approach others with compassion, knowing that ultimate judgment belongs to Yahweh alone. It reminds us that true justice is rooted in righteousness and truth, and that our discernment must be exercised with humility and an awareness of divine standards. We are called not only to distinguish between good and evil, but to do so with a heart aligned with divine justice. In conclusion, discernment is a vital faculty that allows us to navigate life wisely. Yet, it is essential to recognize the divine distinction that Yahweh makes. His discrimination is based on righteousness, justice, and love. This divine discrimination is a model for our own moral discernment and a reminder that justice, when rooted in divine principles, transcends human prejudice. As we seek to understand and emulate Yahweh's justice, may we cultivate discernment that reflects His divine nature which includes discriminating rightly, judging righteously, and loving unconditionally.

Goodwill is an enduring and heartfelt desire to see others flourish, to see them find happiness, peace, and fulfillment in their lives. At its core, goodwill is rooted in a genuine kindness that extends beyond superficial gestures and reaches into the very essence of how we see and treat others. It is born from a kindhearted spirit, a sincere belief in the inherent worth of every person and a compassionate understanding of their struggles, hopes, and dreams.

Having goodwill means more than just acting kindly from time to time, it requires a consistent, sincere effort to uplift those around us. It involves listening with an open heart and offering support without expecting anything in return. When we approach others with genuine compassion, we acknowledge their pain, their joys, and their humanity. This compassion fuels our actions and reminds us that everyone deserves kindness, understanding, and respect, regardless of their circumstances.

A kindhearted person sees beyond superficial differences or missteps and recognizes the potential for goodness in others. They understand that everyone is fighting battles unseen and that a simple act of kindness can make a significant difference. Whether it's offering words of encouragement, lending a helping hand, or just being present and attentive, the kindhearted are driven by an authentic desire to help others feel valued and loved.

True goodwill is rooted in a sincere wish for others' well-being. It is not motivated by personal gain or recognition but by a genuine care for the happiness and health of others. This kind of thinking fosters a more compassionate and harmonious community, where people feel safe to be themselves and supported in their journeys. It's about putting ourselves in others' shoes, understanding their experiences, and responding with kindness from the depths of our hearts.

Living with goodwill also means practicing patience and forgiveness. It recognizes that everyone makes mistakes, and that growth often comes through understanding and compassion rather than judgment. It involves a conscious effort to see the good in others and to believe in their capacity for change and improvement. When we act with goodwill, we create ripples of kindness that can extend far beyond our immediate circle, inspiring others to act with the same sincerity and care.

In essence, goodwill is a reflection of our deepest values and a testament to our desire to make the world a better place through kindness, compassion, and genuine concern for others. It reminds us that at the heart of every act of kindness is a sincere wish for someone else's happiness. Cultivating goodwill within ourselves can bring a profound sense of fulfillment, knowing that our actions driven by a heartfelt desire for good, can bring light into the lives of others, and foster a more caring, compassionate world.

Why is it important to be good? Understanding the meaning of righteousness is imperative. Being good is essential for leading a meaningful and fulfilling life. It shapes who we are and influences how others perceive us. At the core of goodness lies the idea of standing for what is right, just, and moral. Yahweh, the divine name for God in many customs, symbolizes ultimate goodness and righteousness. Recognizing this connection emphasizes why striving to be good is so vital. Yahweh stands for good. In spiritual and moral terms, Yahweh embodies purity, justice, and compassion. His example sets a standard for us to follow. When we aim to be good, we align ourselves with these divine qualities, upholding integrity and moral strength. Being good isn't just about personal merit. It affects our society and the world. Goodness encourages trust, respect, and harmony among humanity. It helps build relationships based on honesty and kindness. In contrast, neglecting goodness leads to chaos, mistrust, and suffering. Moreover, striving to be good is a reflection of Yahweh's values and character. It requires discipline, awareness, and a commitment to doing what is right, even when it's hard. Recognizing that Yahweh stands for good reminds us that our actions have weight beyond ourselves. They contribute to a higher purpose fixed in divine righteousness. In summary, being good is crucial because it aligns us with Yahweh's principles, promotes harmony, and defines our character. Yahweh's embodiment of right-mindedness serves as a guiding light, bolstering the importance of uprightness in our lives. Choose morality continually— for yourself, for others, and for the greater good.

Chapter 3

Throughout history and in every culture, the power of example has proven to be one of the most effective ways to influence others. Our actions often speak louder than words, shaping the hearts and minds of those around us in profound ways. As followers of Yahweh, we are called not only to live uprightly but also to be positive influencers. We are to be beacons of integrity, kindness, and faith that inspire others to walk a righteous path. Yahweh, the Creator of all, desires His children to be lights in the world. He wants us to reflect His goodness, His love, and His justice in our daily lives. When we set a good example, we honor Him and become His instruments of influence. Our lives are a testimony to His transformative power, and through our actions, others are invited to see His grace at work. The importance of setting an example is rooted in the understanding that people often emulate what they see. Children, friends, colleagues, and even strangers observe how we handle challenges, treat others, and live out our faith. When we choose to act with honesty, humility, compassion, and patience, we demonstrate the values that Yahweh wants His followers to uphold. These qualities are not only admirable but also contagious. They inspire others to adopt the same virtues, creating a ripple effect of goodness and righteousness. Yahweh wants positive influencers. He wants people who intentionally live out their faith in a way that uplifts others. This means being consistent in our words and actions, especially in difficult circumstances. When we face trials and still demonstrate trust in Yahweh, forgiveness, and perseverance, we provide a powerful example of faith in action. Such conduct encourages others to trust in Yahweh's plan and to persevere through their own struggles.

Moreover, leading by example involves humility. It's about genuine living that points others toward Yahweh, and recognizing that our strength and wisdom come from Him. When we acknowledge this humility, we motivate others to seek Yahweh's guidance and to live with integrity. Our sincerity in living out our faith creates a trustworthy environment that invites others to explore and embrace the love of Yahweh.

Yahweh also desires us to be influencers of peace and reconciliation. In a world often marred by division and conflict, showing forgiveness, understanding, and love can be transformative. When we choose to act with grace rather than revenge, patience rather than anger, we demonstrate the character of Yahweh. Such actions have the power to heal wounds and to foster unity, inspiring others to follow suit.

It's important to remember that setting an example is a continuous journey. We will stumble and falter at times, but Yahweh's grace is sufficient. The key is to sincerely repent, learn, and renew our commitment to live in a way that honors Him. Our authenticity in striving to be better influences others more than perfect actions ever could.

If we seek to influence others positively, the most effective way is to set an example that reflects the heart of Yahweh. Our lives should be a living testimony of His love, mercy, and righteousness. When we act with integrity, humility, and compassion, we become true positive influencers. We become people through whom Yahweh's light can shine brightly. As we walk this path, let us remember that our influence can spark transformation, inspire hope, and help others see the beauty of living in alignment with Yahweh's will. Ultimately, by setting a godly example, we fulfill Yahweh's desire for His followers to be His ambassadors of goodness and grace in this world. Now on to the word "sway", sometimes simply defined as the power to influence or alter the course of events. This word goes far beyond overt actions and visible outcomes. It embodies a subtle, often intangible force that can shape thoughts, feelings, and decisions in ways that are not immediately apparent. At its core, swaying is about the capacity to bring about change, although not necessarily just through force or direct intervention, but through a gentle and persistent influence that seeps into the very fabric of perceptions and beliefs.

In our daily lives, swaying manifests everywhere. It is present in the quiet confidence of a mentor whose words inspire a student to pursue a dream, or in the empathetic tone of a friend that shifts someone's mood from despair to hope. It resides in the understated power of persuasion like those moments when a well-chosen phrase or a simple gesture gently steers someone's attitude or perspective without a single outright command. This kind of influence often feels less like control and more like a shared movement, a dance in which both parties are subtly affected by each other's presence. The power of "sway" is deeply rooted in the art of understanding and connection. When we seek to bring about change through "sway", we tap into the human longing for recognition, belonging, and hope. We aim to foster trust, build empathy, and foster a sense of possibility. Such influence is indirect, often operating beneath the surface of conscious awareness, yet over time it can lead to profound transformation. A person might start by questioning a belief and gradually come to see things differently, sometimes without even realizing what has shifted. This is the quiet force of "sway" at work, shaping minds and hearts in the most gentle, enduring ways.

Importantly, "sway" is not inherently manipulative or deceptive. When rooted in sincerity and genuine intention, it becomes a powerful tool for positive change. It allows ideas to resonate deeply, creating a ripple effect that extends beyond the initial interaction. Through patience and empathy, we can use sway to inspire action, cultivate understanding, and foster growth, both in ourselves and others. It offers a path to influence that respects individual agency while encouraging openness to new perspectives.

Bringing about change through sway requires subtlety and humility. It involves listening more than speaking, understanding more than convincing, and planting seeds of possibility rather than forcing outcomes. It recognizes that true influence is often a shared journey, an invitation rather than an imposition. When wielded with integrity, sway becomes a gentle but persistent current that guides individuals and communities toward better futures, one thoughtful step at a time.

Ultimately, sway is about the immense capacity we hold to shape the intangible: Our perceptions, our hopes, and our collective spirit. It reminds us that change does not always need to be loud or forceful. Sometimes, it is most powerful when it flows quietly, shaping lives in unseen but profound ways. In embracing the power of sway, we acknowledge the profound impact of subtle influence. It is an enduring, compassionate force that brings about meaningful change in the most intangible of ways. Throughout history, the concept of authority has played a pivotal role in shaping societies, guiding behaviors, and establishing order. At its core, authority is the power to influence the minds and actions of others. It is a force that can inspire, direct, or sometimes constrain human behavior. While authority can be rooted in laws, traditions, or institutions, its most profound impact lies in the subtle yet powerful ability to sway perceptions and choices.

Authority is, in essence, the capacity to influence not just what people do, but what they believe and value. It is an element deeply intertwined with trust, respect, and often, a sense of legitimacy. When individuals recognize and accept authority, they often do so because they believe that the authority figure possesses expertise, moral right, or a justifiable position of power. This recognition creates a psychological influence that guides behavior, often without coercion or force. It is this influence over the mind which controls our beliefs, attitudes, and perceptions that makes authority so compelling and enduring.

The exertion of power over minds is a subtle art. It involves more than just issuing commands; it requires the ability to connect on a level that resonates emotionally and intellectually. Leaders, teachers, parents, and anyone in a position of influence understand that their authority is often rooted in trust and credibility. When people believe in the integrity or competence of an authority figure, they are more likely to internalize their guidance and act accordingly. This internalization is a testament to the true power of influence, shaping not just immediate actions, but long-term attitudes and values.

Authority's influence extends into the realms of societal norms and moral standards. It helps establish what is accepted as right or wrong, shaping collective consciousness and social cohesion. For example, legal authorities influence behavior by establishing rules and consequences, but they also shape perceptions of justice, equity, and order. Similarly, cultural or religious authorities influence the moral compass of individuals, guiding their choices and perceptions of what is meaningful or sacred.

However, the power to influence must be wielded responsibly. When authority is abused or used manipulatively, it can undermine trust and erode the very foundation of influence. Genuine authority, built on authenticity, consistency, and respect, nurtures voluntary compliance and fosters a sense of shared purpose. It recognizes the autonomy of individuals while guiding them toward common goals.

In a sincere pursuit of authority's power to influence, it is essential to understand that true influence is rooted in understanding and empathy. It is about engaging minds and hearts, inspiring confidence, and encouraging individuals to see reasons for their actions that align with their deepest values. Such influence does not diminish freedom; rather, it uplifts and directs it toward positive outcomes.

Authority is more than just a formal position or title. It is the subtle yet potent power to shape the perceptions, beliefs, and behaviors of others. When exercised with integrity, it can foster trust, inspire growth, and create meaningful change. The power to influence through authority is, ultimately, a profound responsibility. It is a power that requires sincerity, humility, and a genuine desire to serve the greater good. In a world where corruption often finds its roots in greed and the desire for personal gain, it is vital to remember the sacred call to integrity and righteousness. Yahweh, the Almighty, is vehemently against bribes, for they distort justice, corrupt the heart, and undermine the moral fabric that binds society together. His stance is clear: to be truly righteous, one must remain incorruptible.

To be incorruptible is to stand firm against the temptations that seek to compromise our morals. It is to resist the trap of bribes, whether they come disguised as favors, gifts, or subtle manipulations. When we accept a bribe, we betray our conscience and distort the truth, putting personal benefit above justice and righteousness. Such acts not only harm others but also diminish our integrity before Yahweh. We must understand that corruption begins with small compromises. A single act of accepting a bribe may seem insignificant at first, but it slowly erodes our moral foundation. The path of corruption is slippery, and once we indulge in it, we distance ourselves from the principles that Yahweh has set forth. To remain incorruptible, we need to guard our hearts and minds vigilantly, recognizing that our integrity is a precious gift from the Divine.

Yahweh commands us to be honest, transparent, and just in all our dealings. He cares deeply about the purity of our hearts and the sincerity of our actions. When we choose to do what is right, even when it is difficult or unpopular, we honor His laws and reflect His character. An incorruptible person is one who refuses to be swayed by greed or pressure; they stand as a beacon of truth and righteousness amidst a fallen world. Furthermore, being incorruptible is not merely about avoiding wrongdoings; it is about actively pursuing goodness and justice. It entails making conscious choices to uphold equity, to speak the truth, and to act with integrity even when nobody is watching. It is a testament to one's devotion to Yahweh and a reflection of His holiness working within us. The strength to remain incorruptible comes from a deep relationship with Yahweh. Prayer, meditation on His Word, and reliance on His Spirit empower us to resist temptation. When we remind ourselves of His righteous standards and the eternal consequences of our actions, we gain the courage to say no to bribes and to uphold truth. We must also surround ourselves with others who share our commitment to integrity, for community support and reinforces our resolve. Let us remember that Yahweh is against bribes because they corrupt the soul and distort justice. To honor Him, we must strive to be incorruptible, living lives marked by honesty, integrity, and unwavering commitment to what is right.

Do not corrupt yourself for fleeting gains, for your true worth lies in your fidelity to Yahweh's standards. In remaining pure and honest, we not only honor Him but also contribute to a just and righteous society. May we always choose integrity over corruption, standing firm as witnesses of His truth and His righteousness. Weight is often perceived merely as a measure of mass, a numerical value representing how heavy an object is. Yet, beneath this simple definition lies a profound metaphor for the overpowering force that can shape our hearts, our decisions, and our relationships. In the realm of human connection and goodwill, weight becomes an emblem of influence. It is an intangible yet deeply impactful force capable of transforming hostility into harmony, indifference into understanding, and separation into unity.

At first glance, weight might seem to symbolize burden or responsibility. Indeed, life often assigns us heavy burdens which bring forth doubts, regrets, and hardships that test our resilience. But within this heaviness lies an extraordinary power: The capacity to evoke empathy, compassion, and ultimately, goodwill. When we carry our own weights with sincerity and humility, we demonstrate an overpowering force that encourages others to see our genuine intentions. Our willingness to bear burdens openly and vulnerably can inspire others to do the same, fostering a collective strength rooted in understanding and mutual respect.

The true power of weight manifests in its ability to influence hearts beyond superficial interactions. Think of moments when a single act (perhaps a kind word or a simple gesture) carries the weight of sincerity, overwhelming cynicism with kindness. Such acts, infused with authentic intent, wield an overpowering force that can dissolve barriers and ignite trust. When someone recognizes that another's actions are genuine, their hesitations falter, replaced by a newfound goodwill. It's as if the weight of kindness becomes an unstoppable force, pushing away negativity and making space for reconciliation and harmony. Furthermore, weight has a compelling influence in the realm of forgiveness and reconciliation.

The heavy realization of past mistakes and hurts can serve as a catalyst for change. When individuals acknowledge the weight of their actions, they often feel an overpowering urge to make amends, to heal wounds and restore trust. This acknowledgment is not merely a burden; It is a force that compels us to act with sincerity, to mend broken bonds, and to build bridges where walls once stood. In this way, weight becomes an agent of goodwill. It becomes an overpowering force that leads us toward compassion and understanding. In relationships, the weight of shared experiences, struggles, and triumphs creates a profound bond. The more genuinely we carry the weight of others' feelings and histories, the more we demonstrate an overpowering force of empathy. It is this empathy that fosters goodwill. It is an unspoken understanding that we are not isolated beings, but interconnected souls navigating life's complex terrain together. When we recognize the weight others carry and respond with kindness, we activate a powerful force capable of transforming individual interactions into lasting bonds of trust and affection.

The significance of weight as an overpowering force also extends to the larger community and society. When individuals and groups take responsibility for their collective burdens whether it's social injustice, environmental challenges, or economic disparity, their unified effort can be an unstoppable force for positive change. The weight of shared purpose and moral conviction can overwhelm apathy and indifference, inspiring collective action rooted in goodwill. It's a reminder that meaningful change often begins when enough people recognize the weight of an issue and choose to respond with compassion and resolve.

Ultimately, the true strength of weight lies in its capacity to cause goodwill, not through domination or coercion, but through the sincere acknowledgment of our shared humanity. It is an overpowering force that compels us to look beyond ourselves, to see others' burdens as opportunities for connection, and to respond with kindness that can move mountains of misunderstanding. When we carry our own weight with integrity and extend that same sincerity to others, we unleash an unstoppable force rooted in love, compassion, and genuine goodwill that can transform individuals, communities, and the world.

In the end, weight is not just a measure of how heavy an object is. It is a profound symbol of the power we hold within, the power to influence hearts and minds through authentic and sincere gestures. It is an overpowering force that, when wielded with kindness and understanding, can forge a world where goodwill prevails, and humanity rises above its divisions. Let us recognize the weight we carry and use it wisely, for in doing so, we harness an incredible force capable of shaping a better tomorrow. In our pursuit of meaning and purpose, one concept consistently emerges as a guiding principle: leverage. The idea of leverage is often associated with business or finance, using a small amount of effort to achieve a disproportionately large impact. Yet at its core, leverage is about power, including how we harness our resources, principles, and moral compass to effect meaningful change. When we consider what Yahweh desires for us, we find that leverage takes on a profound moral dimension, emphasizing that true effectiveness is rooted in moral efficacy.

Yahweh, in His wisdom, desires for us to cultivate moral efficacy—the ability to do good, to influence positively, and to embody righteousness in our actions. This is not merely about personal virtue but about engaging the world in a way that elevates others and advances justice. When we speak of leverage in this divine context, we are talking about the strategic and intentional use of our moral resources to bring about Yahweh's purposes on earth. Moral efficacy begins with understanding that our actions matter. Every decision, no matter how small, carries weight. When driven by a sincere desire to align with Yahweh's will, our efforts become leverage points for His kingdom. For instance, demonstrating integrity in our work, showing compassion to those in need, or standing firm against injustice all are ways in which we leverage our moral standing to effect positive change. But why does Yahweh emphasize moral efficacy? Because effectiveness rooted in morality is sustainable and impactful. Unlike superficial success that can fade or cause harm, moral efficacy builds trust, cultivates genuine relationships, and fosters lasting change. It transforms leverage from a mere tool for personal gain into a divine instrument for good. When our efforts are guided by Yahweh's moral principles such as justice, mercy, humility, love, we operate with a divine leverage that amplifies our impact beyond what is immediately visible.

Furthermore, Yahweh's desire for moral efficacy challenges us to consider the source of our leverage. It's not merely about what we can do on our own but about how we align ourselves with divine guidance. When we seek Yahweh's wisdom and follow His commandments, we tap into a higher form of leverage, a supernatural efficacy that enables us to overcome obstacles and influence situations in ways we could not achieve alone. This divine leverage empowers us to be agents of transformation, bringing Yahweh's light into darkness.

In practical terms, cultivating moral efficacy and leveraging it effectively requires humility, vigilance, and intentionality. It involves daily choices including acting honestly when no one is watching, speaking truthfully, advocating for the oppressed, forgiving those who have wronged us, and living out the love of Yahweh. These acts, seemingly small, accumulate and create ripple effects that can transform communities and nations when guided by Yahweh's moral standards.

The path to moral efficacy also involves recognizing our limitations and seeking divine strength. We are finite beings, but Yahweh's power is infinite. When we acknowledge our dependence on Him and invite His guidance, our leverage becomes multiplied. It is no longer solely dependent on our own abilities but infused with divine power. This is the essence of spiritual leverage: aligning our efforts with Yahweh's purposes to maximize effectiveness for His glory.

The divine concept of leverage, as it relates to Yahweh's desire for moral efficacy, calls us to intentionality and integrity. It urges us to see our actions as strategic opportunities to influence and serve in accordance with Yahweh's moral will. When we leverage our lives through the lens of righteousness, love, and justice, we tap into a divine effectiveness that transcends human limitations. Our efforts, rooted in moral efficacy, become powerful instruments in Yahweh's hand, bringing about lasting change, advancing His kingdom, and reflecting His glory. Let us therefore seek to harness this divine leverage, knowing that through it, our lives can achieve effectivity that eternally matters.

In these moments, the question of whether we have the strength, or ability to act, or whether we possess the "might" becomes a pressing concern. But what if our true power does not originate solely from within us, but from a divine source that sustains and empowers us? What if the very ability to produce an effect, to act with purpose and conviction, is a gift bestowed by Yahweh?

Yahweh, the Creator of all, is continually extending His power to His children. His might is not limited or diminishing; rather, it is abundant and enduring. It is through His grace that we find the strength to face life's difficulties, to stand firm against adversity, and to carry out acts of kindness, justice, and love. When we acknowledge that our capacity to act comes from Yahweh, our perspective shifts. No longer do we rely solely on our own limited strength, but we recognize that our ability to make a difference flows from a divine source.

In the Scriptures, we see numerous examples of Yahweh granting power to His people. Moses, who once felt unworthy and hesitant, was empowered by Yahweh's mighty hand to lead the Israelites out of bondage. David, a young shepherd boy, was given the might to face Goliath, not just through his own courage, but through faith in Yahweh's provision. The prophets, the leaders, and even ordinary individuals found their acts of courage and righteousness rooted in the strength that Yahweh supplied.

This divine empowerment is not just about heroic feats or grand gestures; it is also about the daily acts of love, patience, and perseverance. When we serve others, forgive those who wrong us, stand up for what is right, or simply endure hardships with hope, we are demonstrating the might that Yahweh grants. His power is made perfect in our weakness, as the Apostle Paul reminds us, and it is in our reliance on Him that our actions become effective and meaningful.

Understanding that Yahweh gives us power also brings humility and gratitude. It humbles us to realize that our capacity to act is not solely a product of our own effort or intelligence but a reflection of His divine favor and strength. Gratitude flows from this recognition, inspiring us to use the power given to us responsibly, for the good of others and for His glory.

Furthermore, the promise of divine might assures us that we are never truly alone or powerless. In moments of doubt or fear, we can turn to Yahweh in prayer, seeking His strength to continue, to act, and to produce positive effects in our lives and the lives of those around us. His might sustains us when our own strength fails, and His power works through us to accomplish what we could not do on our own. In embracing this truth, we become more than just individuals trying to get by; we become vessels of divine power, called to act with purpose and conviction. Whether in small acts of kindness or in large endeavors of justice, we carry the might of the Creator within us. This divine empowerment transforms our capabilities, enabling us to produce effects that have eternal significance. Let us, therefore, walk humbly and confidently, knowing that Yahweh, in His infinite love and power, gives us the might to act. May we use this gift wisely, with hearts full of gratitude and a desire to serve others, trusting that through His strength, we can make a difference. For in Him, our ability to produce an effect is not limited by our own capacity, but amplified by His boundless might.

In the sacred pursuit of creating a just and righteous society, we hereby establish this Code of Laws, rooted in the divine statutes and commandments handed down by Yahweh, the Eternal Creator. Let this be a solemn declaration that our foundation shall be built upon unwavering fidelity to His will, guiding our actions, our judgments, and our collective purpose. We acknowledge Yahweh as the Sovereign one and the ultimate authority over all creation. Our laws are derived from His divine commandments, which serve as the moral compass for our community. We commit ourselves to follow His statutes diligently, recognizing that adherence to His laws sustains justice, peace, and righteousness among us. The establishment of our society shall be a reflection of our devotion to Yahweh, honoring His name, and living according to His divine principles. The statutes of Yahweh are eternal and unchanging. They serve as the blueprint for a life of integrity and humility. We shall teach these statutes diligently to our children, ensuring that each generation understands and values the sacred laws given by our Creator. The statutes encompass both ceremonial rites and moral directives, including love, mercy, justice, and humility. Ignorance of these statutes shall not be an excuse. Instead, we shall seek understanding through study, prayer, and reflection.

Justice is divine, therefore, our judgments must mirror Yahweh's righteousness. Judges appointed among us shall be wise, impartial, and grounded in the fear of Yahweh, ensuring that every case is judged with equity and truth. No partiality shall influence judgment; the weak and the strong, the rich and the poor, shall receive equal justice under the laws of Yahweh. We recognize that judgment is both a divine and a communal duty to uphold righteousness and to correct injustice whenever it appears. The 613 Laws, Statues, Judgements and Commandments are the cornerstone of our moral code. They shall serve as the guiding principles for individual conduct and societal harmony. We shall honor Yahweh's name, keep His Shabbath, and refrain from idolatry, respecting His sovereignty over our lives. We shall honor our parents and elders, recognizing their role in guiding the community in righteousness. We shall uphold honesty, refrain from theft and falsehood, and pursue justice and peace in all our dealings. Our community shall be a reflection of Yahweh's love, mercy, and righteousness. Our establishment is not merely a legal framework but a heartfelt covenant with Yahweh. Our sincerity in following His laws shall be evident in our actions and intentions. We acknowledge that human weakness may lead us astray; therefore, repentance, forgiveness, and continuous striving to align with Yahweh's will are essential. Our laws shall be enforced with compassion and humility, recognizing that the path to righteousness is a journey shared by all members of our society. We commit to fostering an environment where truth, justice, and faith flourish, strengthening our bonds as a community dedicated to Yahweh's divine plan. This code of laws, statues, judgements and commandments is a living document, rooted in the eternal covenant we establish with Yahweh. As we uphold His laws, statutes, judgments, and commandments, we reaffirm our devotion and obedience to His sacred will. We shall remember that our establishment is a testimony to Yahweh's glory and a beacon of His righteousness in the world. Our sincerity in maintaining this covenant shall inspire future generations to walk in His light, ensuring that His laws, statutes, judgments, and commandments endure forever. May this Code of Establishment serve as a sacred guide, a testament to our sincere commitment to follow Yahweh's laws, statutes, judgments, and commandments. May our society be founded on divine truth, justice, and love, so that we may flourish under His gracious guidance and fulfill our divine purpose with humility and devotion.

Let all who hear these words be reminded that our true strength lies in obedience to the Creator Yahweh, and our lasting peace is found in faithfully walking His righteous path. Mastery is often seen as the pinnacle of achievement in any field, a state where one's skill or knowledge transcends ordinary understanding and becomes an intrinsic part of one's being. It is not merely about accumulating information or honing technical skills, it is about cultivating a deep, unwavering connection to the core principles that define a subject, and in doing so, elevating oneself to a level of true mastery. At its heart, mastery involves relentless dedication, humility, patience, and a sincere desire to grow beyond limitations.

To understand mastery in its fullest sense, one must recognize that it isn't an endpoint but a continual journey of learning, refining, and deepening. It is about immersing oneself fully in the subject, developing an intuitive understanding that guides actions and decisions seamlessly. When one masters a skill or knowledge, their actions often appear effortless, yet behind that ease is countless hours of practice, reflection, and unwavering commitment. True mastery is humility dressed in confidence. It recognizes that there is always more to learn and that each step forward brings new insights and challenges. A crucial aspect of mastery that often goes unnoticed is mastering righteousness. Righteousness, in this context, refers to understanding and embodying what is morally right, just, and ethical. It is about aligning one's actions with a sense of integrity that transcends personal gain or superficial success. To master righteousness is to cultivate a moral compass that guides every decision, every interaction, and every pursuit. It is about embodying virtues such as honesty, compassion, equity, and humility in a way that naturally influences others and elevates one's character. Mastering righteousness requires sincere effort and a deep commitment to integrity. It involves recognizing the importance of doing what is right not just outwardly, but from a genuine conviction within. It is a continuous process of self-examination, learning from mistakes, and striving to improve oneself morally. This mastery does not come from mere knowledge of rules or principles; rather, it comes from internalizing these values so thoroughly that they become a natural part of one's character. When one masters righteousness, their actions reflect their true principles, even in difficult circumstances.

Furthermore, mastering righteousness enriches one's mastery of any subject because it adds depth, purpose, and authenticity to one's pursuits. When mastery is rooted in righteousness, it is not hollow achievement but a meaningful journey that benefits oneself and others. It cultivates trust, respect, and goodwill, which are the true foundations of enduring mastery. Such mastery ensures that success is not achieved at the expense of moral integrity, but rather through actions that uplift and inspire. Mastery is a profound and lifelong pursuit that encompasses more than technical skill or knowledge. It involves developing a deep understanding and command of a subject, guided by principles of righteousness. To master righteousness is to embody moral virtues in all aspects of life, ensuring that one's mastery is authentic, sustainable, and truly impactful. It calls for sincere dedication, humility, and a genuine desire to grow morally and intellectually. Ultimately, mastery rooted in righteousness transforms not only the individual but also the world around them, fostering a legacy of integrity, virtue, and genuine excellence. Self-control is a vital virtue that guides us in exercising restraint and directing our influence over ourselves and others. It is the foundation upon which our character is built and often the measure of our integrity and strength of purpose. Cultivating self-control is not merely about suppressing impulses; it is about intentionally choosing the right course of action, especially when it is difficult or inconvenient. When we exercise self-control, we demonstrate our respect for others, our commitment to righteousness, and our desire to live in accordance with divine principles.

In the eyes of Yahweh, our actions are a reflection of our inner character. He observes not only what we do but also the intentions behind our deeds. One of the most profound ways to honor Yahweh is to do right by others. This includes showing kindness, patience, and equity. Self-control plays a crucial role in this because it empowers us to respond with love rather than anger, patience instead of frustration, and understanding rather than judgment. It allows us to be consistent in our words and actions, aligning ourselves with the moral standards set forth in Scripture. Being an example of self-control is a powerful testimony to others and a way of glorifying Yahweh.

When we choose to exercise restraint in moments of temptation or provocation, we demonstrate the strength of our faith and the influence of His Spirit working within us. These acts of discipline help build trust and respect in our relationships with people and with the Creator Yahweh. They serve as a living testament to the transformation that comes through genuine obedience and commitment to His commandments.

Self-control also involves the deliberate steering of our influence. Our words, attitudes, and behaviors can either uplift or diminish those around us. By exercising restraint, we avoid causing unnecessary hurt and instead foster an environment of peace and understanding. This is especially important in our interactions with family, friends, colleagues, and even strangers. When we master ourselves, we become better ambassadors of Yahweh's love and grace.

It's important to remember that self-control is not about denying ourselves joy or satisfaction but about managing our desires in a way that honors Yahweh and benefits others. It requires humility, patience, and reliance on His strength. Daily, we are faced with choices like how to respond to provocations, how to handle our frustrations, and how to manage our impulses. Each decision to exercise restraint is a step toward becoming more Yahweh-like, reflecting His patience, kindness, and self-discipline.

Moreover, developing self-control is a lifelong journey. It involves recognizing our weaknesses, seeking forgiveness when we stumble, and continually striving to improve. Prayer, meditation on Scripture, and accountability with fellow believers can help us stay anchored and motivated. Remember, Yahweh's mercy is sufficient for us, and His Spirit empowers us to overcome our fleshly tendencies.

Exercising self-control is a powerful demonstration of our love for Yahweh and our desire to live righteously. It reminds us that our influence extends beyond ourselves and that our conduct can be a light in a dark world. By being examples of restraint and directing our influence toward goodness and kindness, we honor Yahweh's name and become instruments of His peace.

Let us commit each day to practicing self-control, not out of obligation alone, but out of genuine love for Yahweh and reverence for His commands. Through this, we not only grow in character but also draw others closer to the divine truth that sets us free. Throughout history, the concept of rule has often been associated with power, authority, and control. Yet, true leadership is not merely about holding a position of dominance or commanding obedience. It is about wielding influence in a way that aligns with higher principles, virtues, and divine expectations. To have power over others is a profound responsibility. It is one that must be exercised with humility, integrity, and a sincere commitment to righteousness, especially in the eyes of Yahweh.

Ruling righteously begins with understanding that authority is a trust bestowed by the Creator Yahweh. As leaders, whether in personal relationships, communities, or nations, our legitimacy is not derived solely from laws, traditions, or even societal approval, but from our obedience to divine commandments. Yahweh, the righteous Judge, calls us to lead with justice, compassion, and equity. When we govern according to His standards, we fulfill our role in aligning worldly authority with divine will.

To rule righteously in Yahweh's eyes requires a sincere heart dedicated to humility. Power can tempt even the most well-intentioned leaders to become prideful or oppressive. But true rulership is marked by a willingness to serve others instead of seeking personal gain or recognition. It involves listening to the voices of the oppressed, seeking justice for the vulnerable, and making decisions that reflect love and mercy. In this, the leader recognizes that all authority is ultimately from above, and that their power is a stewardship, not an entitlement.

Furthermore, righteousness in rule calls for unwavering integrity. Leaders must be honest, transparent, and consistent in their actions. Deception, corruption, and unjust practices tarnish not only the leader's reputation but also undermine the very foundation of righteous rule. When a leader's conduct aligns with Yahweh's commandments such as loving your neighbor, practicing honesty, or promoting peace, they establish a governance rooted in divine truth. Such integrity inspires trust and respect, which are essential for genuine authority.

It is also vital to remember that ruling righteously involves a continuous pursuit of wisdom and discernment. Yahweh values humility in seeking guidance and understanding from Him. Praying for wisdom and consulting divine principles ensures that decisions are made with justice and compassion. Righteous rulers do not rely solely on human knowledge or personal opinions, they seek divine insight to lead with equity and humility.

Moreover, righteous rule reflects a deep commitment to justice. Justice is not simply about enforcing laws but about ensuring equity and impartiality for all. It means defending the rights of the marginalized, punishing wrongdoing without bias, and cultivating an environment where righteousness can flourish. When rulers prioritize divine justice over personal or political interests, they honor Yahweh's standards and foster peace and stability.

Finally, ruling in Yahweh's eyes demands sincerity, an authentic devotion to the principles of righteousness, humility, and love. It is easy to adopt a facade of authority, but true rulership is about inner conviction and a genuine desire to serve others according to divine commandments. Leaders must continually examine their motives, heart, and actions, seeking forgiveness and correction when they fall short. To have power over others is a significant responsibility that requires more than authority. It necessitates righteousness rooted in a sincere, humble desire to serve according to Yahweh's will. Ruling righteously in the eyes of Yahweh is about embodying justice, integrity, humility, and compassion. It is a calling to lead others not for personal glory, but for the greater good, always mindful that true power is exercised when aligned with divine standards. Only then can a leader truly have power over others that is just, righteous, and pleasing in the sight of Yahweh. Restraint is a virtue that often goes unnoticed in a world that celebrates boldness, impulsiveness, and unrestrained expression. Yet, it is precisely in the quiet, deliberate act of controlling our emotions and thoughts that true strength resides.

Restraint is not about suppressing our feelings or denying our humanity. Rather, it is about choosing to exercise mastery over ourselves, especially in moments of chaos or temptation. It is an acknowledgment that our responses have power, not just over ourselves, but also over the impact we have on others and our relationship with the divine.

In many spiritual traditions, including the Hebrew faith, restraint holds a special place. To the children of Yahweh, self-control is not merely a personal attribute but a reflection of inner discipline rooted in reverence for Yahweh. The Scriptures often stress that true devotion involves more than outward actions; it calls for a heart that exercises restraint, especially in times of anger, desire, or temptation. See Case Law § **Proverbs 16:32** states, "*He that is* slow to anger *is* better than the mighty; and he that ruleth his spirit than he that taketh a city.*" This verse highlights that strength is not solely measured by outer conquests but by the ability to govern one's own passions.

From Yahweh's perspective, restraint is an act of humility and worship. It recognizes that our human impulses can lead us astray, and it honors the divine order by choosing patience and moderation. When we exercise restraint, we acknowledge that we are not the ultimate masters of ourselves; rather, we submit to a higher authority that guides us toward righteousness. The Lord Yahweh desires His followers to reflect His own restraint, His patience in bearing with our flaws, His mercy in forgiving our sins, as well as His enduring love that does not rush to judgment.

The example of Yahweh's restraint is evident throughout scripture. Yahweh's dealings with humanity often show profound patience and long-suffering. He is slow to anger see Case Law § **Nahum 1:3**, waiting patiently for us to turn back to Him, offering forgiveness rather than immediate punishment. This divine restraint is a testament to His love and mercy, setting a standard for His followers to emulate. When we exercise restraint in our own lives whether in words, actions, or thoughts, we mirror the divine character and demonstrate our trust in Yahweh's wisdom and timing.

Self-restraint also requires honesty and humility. It entails recognizing our vulnerabilities, acknowledging moments when our passions threaten to override our better judgment, and deliberately choosing restraint despite the allure of immediate gratification. It is a daily, sometimes hourly, conscious decision to align our actions with our values and our faith. Such discipline is not easy, it demands effort, patience, and often, the grace of Yahweh. Yet, it is through this discipline that we grow closer to the likeness of Yahweh, who exemplified perfect restraint and humility.

Furthermore, restraint fosters peace, not only within ourselves but also in our relationships with others. When we exercise control over our emotions, we prevent conflicts from escalating and create an environment of understanding and compassion. This is especially important in a society that often encourages reactive behavior. By practicing restraint, we become witnesses to the transformative power of self-control, demonstrating that strength is rooted in patience and humility rather than in impulsiveness or dominance.

In the eyes of Yahweh, restraint is a reflection of true faith, a trust that His plan is best and that sometimes, the wisest course of action is to hold back, to listen before speaking, to forgive instead of retaliating. It signifies a deep trust in divine sovereignty and a recognition that we are called to live differently from the world's patterns—patterns of excess, anger, and haste.

Restraint is a sacred discipline that connects us to the divine and elevates our character. It is an act of surrender, a recognition that our strength is not in our impulses but in our ability to choose love, patience, and humility. In the eyes of Yahweh, self-control is a vital expression of faith and a testament to our understanding that true power lies in the mastery of oneself. As we strive to cultivate restraint in our daily lives, we honor Yahweh's desire for us to be measured, gentle, and disciplined, reflecting His own infinite patience and mercy.

Chapter 4

In a world filled with countless distractions, influences, and pressures, the call to stand our ground has never been more vital. To stand our ground is not merely about resistance or stubbornness; it is about a deep commitment to control of our own affairs, guided by a sincere desire to live in accordance with divine principles. At the heart of true self-governance lies the recognition that we are accountable to Yahweh, the Creator of all, who calls us to lead lives marked by integrity, responsibility, and humility. Self-governance begins with understanding that each of us is entrusted with the gift of free will. Yahweh, in His infinite wisdom, grants us the authority to make choices—choices that shape our character, our relationships, and our destiny. To stand our ground is to accept this divine trust and to exercise it thoughtfully, with an awareness that our actions reflect our dedication to Yahweh's laws, statues, judgement and commandments and His love. Living in the eyes of Yahweh means acknowledging that He sees our intentions and motivations even when others do not. It is a call to sincerity, an earnest desire to align our will with Yahweh's divine purpose. When we choose to stand firm in our beliefs, especially in challenging circumstances, we demonstrate a real faith that Yahweh's guidance is steadfast and true. Our steadfastness becomes a testament not only to our moral strength but also to our trust in Yahweh's sovereignty. Self-governance, in this spiritual context, involves cultivating inner discipline, resisting the temptations that drift us away from righteousness, and maintaining integrity despite outer pressures. It is about setting boundaries that honor Yahweh's commands and holding firm to the principles that we believe in, even when it is difficult to do so.

To stand our ground is to refuse to compromise our values for fleeting gains or superficial approval. It is a declaration that our lives belong first and foremost to Yahweh, and that His will guides our decisions. Moreover, standing our ground requires humility. Recognizing that our strength comes from Yahweh and not solely from ourselves fosters a humble confidence. We acknowledge our limitations and seek His wisdom in each step we take. In doing so, we prevent arrogance and pride from undermining our self-governance. Instead, we remain open to Yahweh's correction and mercy, knowing that true strength is placed in dependence on Him. The journey of self-governance in the eyes of Yahweh is ongoing. It involves daily renewal, prayer, reflection, and a sincere desire to grow closer to Him. As we face life's challenges whether they involve moral dilemmas, personal struggles, or outside opposition, standing our ground becomes an act of faith and obedience. It is a testimony to our conviction that Yahweh's truth is more enduring than any fleeting influence or societal trend.

Ultimately, to stand our ground is to embody a life of integrity, anchored in the understanding that our affairs are under divine sovereignty. It is to live in truth, with honesty and courage, trusting that Yahweh honors those who remain faithful to His principles. When we govern ourselves in accordance with Yahweh's will, we not only find peace within but also become haloes of His light for others. Let us remember that true self-governance is a sacred duty, a reflection of our relationship with Yahweh. It demands sincerity, humility, and unwavering resolve to live by His truth. As we stand our ground, may we do so with confidence that we are fulfilling our divine calling, controlled by Yahweh's Spirit and guided by His everlasting love. In this steadfastness, we find the strength to face whatever comes, knowing that we are aligned with the highest Authority and that our lives can be a testimony of Yahweh's goodness and sovereignty. In the journey of life, we are often faced with challenges that seem insurmountable, obstacles that threaten to break our spirit, and situations that test our resolve. It is during these moments that the true measure of our character is revealed. At the core of this resilience lies a profound and divine gift: willpower. This inner strength, rooted in faith and trust, is not merely a human trait but a blessing bestowed upon us by Yahweh, our Creator and Sustainer.

Yahweh, in His infinite wisdom and mercy, has given each of us a spark of divine will, an unwavering determination that can carry us through the darkest valleys and the highest peaks. This gift is not just about stubbornness or mere persistence, it is a sacred force that aligns our spirit with Yahweh's divine purpose. When we draw upon this heavenly endowment, we find a wellspring of strength that surpasses physical endurance or mental resilience. It is a reflection of Yahweh's power within us, a testament to His belief in our capacity to overcome.

The strength of will given by Yahweh is rooted in faith. It is through faith that we recognize that our challenges are not solely ours to bear but are part of a divine plan. When we pray and seek Yahweh's guidance, we fortify our resolve with His divine support. This divine support will empower us to stand firm in the face of adversity, to push beyond our perceived limitations, and to persist when all seems lost. It reminds us that we are not alone. Yahweh's presence is with us, strengthening our resolve and inspiring us to keep moving forward.

Moreover, this divine gift calls us to a higher purpose. It is not merely about personal perseverance but about fulfilling the destiny Yahweh has set for each of us. When we act with unwavering will, guided by His wisdom, we participate in His divine plan. Our perseverance becomes a testament of our faith, a living witness to Yahweh's power working through us. It is this divine will that enables us to do difficult things, not because we are superhuman, but because Yahweh empowers us, His children.

To develop and nurture this divine will, we must remain connected to Yahweh through prayer, reading His Word, and trusting in His promises. Every act of faith, every moment of surrender, reinforces our resolve and reminds us that we are equipped by Yahweh to face any challenges. The more we lean on Yahweh's strength, the more resilient we become. Our determination is no longer solely ours. It is a divine partnership, a synergy of human effort and divine power. In difficult times, when the road ahead seems long and difficult, remember that Yahweh has given you the gift of divine will. Call upon it. Believe in it. Let it fuel your actions and sustain your spirit. Through Yahweh's strength, you can accomplish what once seemed impossible. The obstacles may remain, but with divine will as your foundation, you will find the courage and perseverance to overcome them.

Let this sacred gift inspire you to face life's trials with confidence and humility. Know that Yahweh's will is with you, empowering you to do difficult things. Trust in Yahweh's divine purpose for your life, and step forward with a strong, unwavering heart. Your perseverance, grounded in faith, can move mountains and turn dreams into reality because you are carrying within you the divine will of Yahweh, the greatest source of strength and determination known to the world.

Remember, with Yahweh's will flowing through you, there is nothing you cannot endure, nothing you cannot achieve. Stand firm in His strength, and let your life be a testament to His divine power working through your unwavering will. In a world that is constantly shifting, where values are often compromised, and the pressure to conform is relentless, there is an outright strength in choosing to stand. To stand is more than simply remaining upright physically. It is a declaration of integrity, belief, and unwavering faith. It is a conscious decision to uphold what is right, just, and pure in the eyes of Yahweh, regardless of the circumstances or the opinions of others.

To stand for what is right in Yahweh's eyes is the highest calling of a believer. It is rooted in the understanding that His standards are eternal and unchanging. Unlike fleeting societal trends or popular opinions, Yahweh's commandments and His righteous character serve as a firm foundation upon which we can build our lives. When we stand, we align ourselves with Yahweh's truth, refusing to be swayed by the temptations of compromise or the allure of worldly success at the expense of righteousness.

Standing firm requires sincerity. It involves a heartfelt commitment to live according to Yahweh's commandments, even when it is difficult or unpopular. It means not merely paying lip service to faith, but embodying it through our actions, words, and attitude. A sincere stand is motivated by love for Yahweh and a desire to honor Him in all aspects of life. It is a stand deep in humility, recognizing that our strength comes from Yahweh alone and that our righteousness is a reflection of His mercy working within us.

Throughout Scripture, we see countless examples of individuals who dared to stand for what was right before Yahweh. Noah stood firm in a corrupt generation, faithfully building the ark despite ridicule. Daniel stood unwavering in his devotion to Yahweh, even when faced with the lion's den. Esther courageously stood for her people, risking her own life to intervene. These stories inspire us to remain steadfast, to hold our ground with sincerity and courage, trusting that Yahweh honors those who stand for righteousness.

Maintaining one's position is not always easy. The pressures to conform, to stay silent in the face of injustice, or to neglect our spiritual duties can be overwhelming. Yet, it is precisely in these moments that our true character is revealed. Standing in truth and righteousness is an act of faith, a testimony to the world that Yahweh's standards are worth defending. It reflects our deep trust that His ways are higher, His judgments are just, and His promises are true.

To stand also means to be resilient. It is to endure opposition, rejection, or even persecution with a sincere heart, knowing that Yahweh's approval is far more valuable than worldly acceptance. It is a daily decision to remain committed, to renew our resolve each morning, and to seek Yahweh's strength when our own falters. Prayer, reading His Word, and fellowship with other believers serve as vital supports in our journey to stand firm.

Ultimately, our goal is to maintain our position, not out of stubbornness or pride, but out of genuine love and respect for Yahweh. We stand because we recognize that Yahweh's way is perfect, His commandments are life-giving, and His truth is everlasting. When we stand for what is right in Yahweh's eyes, we serve as beacons of His righteousness in a darkened world. Our sincerity in this stand can inspire others to seek Yahweh's truth and find hope in His righteousness. To stand is to declare our allegiance to Yahweh's truth. It is a sincere act of faith that requires courage, humility, and perseverance.

By standing for what is right in Yahweh's eyes, we affirm our trust in His sovereignty and show our commitment to live according to His divine standards. May we all find the strength to stand firm, unwavering in our conviction, steadfast in our pursuit of righteousness, and knowing that Yahweh honors those who stand for Him with sincerity and love. In life, our actions and commitments often position us on a particular path, one that can lead to gain or loss, blessing or challenge. Among the most profound of these commitments is the decision to stand firm in our faith and allegiance to Yahweh. To stand, in this context, is not merely about physical posture, but about a sincere, unwavering stance rooted in conviction and trust.

Making a commitment to Yahweh is an act of pure sincerity. It is an acknowledgment that our lives are intertwined with divine purpose, and that our allegiance to Yahweh guides every decision we make. When we stand before Yahweh and declare our devotion, we are choosing to align ourselves with His truth and His will. Such a stance is not taken lightly. It is born out of earnest reflection and a heartfelt desire to walk in righteousness. However, standing for Yahweh is not always easy. The world around us often challenges our beliefs, and societal pressures might tempt us to compromise or retreat. In these moments, our stance becomes a test. Will we hold firm in our commitment, or will we waver? It is in these critical junctures that our sincerity is revealed, and where our standing can either lead to spiritual growth and divine blessing or result in loss and discontent if we falter. To make a commitment to Yahweh is to accept the possibility of both gain and loss. The gain manifests in the deepening of our relationship with Him, the peace that surpasses understanding, and the assurance of Yahweh's presence and guidance in our lives. It is an eternal hope that sustains us through difficulties, reminding us that standing firm in Yahweh is ultimately a source of strength and blessing. Conversely, the risk of loss lies in the potential consequences of unwavering allegiance, persecution, misunderstanding, or rejection by others. Yet, true sincerity recognizes that these potential losses pale in comparison to the eternal rewards of faithfully standing with Yahweh. When we commit ourselves wholeheartedly, we are choosing a path that may be narrow and challenging, but ultimately one that leads to total fulfillment and divine favor.

Standing also requires humility and honesty. It is a sincere acknowledgment that, apart from Yahweh's strength, we are vulnerable. Our commitment must be rooted in real faith, not pretentious gestures or passing feelings. It involves daily reaffirmation, renewing our stance through prayer, study, and actions that reflect our devotion.

In the end, standing in commitment to Yahweh is a declaration of our sincerity and determination. It is a choice to be steady in our faith, even when circumstances threaten to undermine us. This stance positions us to experience the fullness of Yahweh's promises whether in victory or in perseverance through trials. Because of this commitment, we are prepared to face whatever comes, confident that our stand is deep in divine truth and that our sincerity will be rewarded.

So, let us take a sincere stand today, pledging our lives anew to Yahweh, knowing that this commitment has the power to shape our destiny. Whether we gain or lose in the worldly sense, we are assured that standing firm in Yahweh is always the right choice. It is a stand that reflects our deepest sincerity and our trust in His everlasting love and sovereignty. In a world that is ever-changing, where trends shift rapidly and values are often compromised, there exists a real call to remain steadfast, especially in our faith and commitment to Yahweh. The thought of validity is not merely about being recognized or accepted by others. It is about enduring through time, maintaining integrity, and bearing fruit that is genuine and efficacious in the eyes of Yahweh.

To stand firm for Yahweh is to acknowledge that His truth is eternal, unchanging, and supreme. It is to recognize that, despite the pressures of societal norms, personal doubts, or outside forces, the core of our faith remains valid because it is rooted in divine authority. Validity, in this context, is not temporary. It is not dependent on popularity or worldly approval but is anchored in the unshakeable foundation of Yahweh's Word and His promises.

Remaining valid in our spiritual walk requires sincerity, a heartfelt commitment that is unwavering. We must cultivate a sincere desire to uphold Yahweh's principles even when it is inconvenient or unpopular. Sincerity means aligning our actions, words, and inner beliefs with the truth of Yahweh's commandments. It is about being genuine in our faith, not merely going through motions to appear righteous but embodying righteousness from within. This sincerity gives our faith its efficacy, allowing it to be a living testimony that influences not just ourselves but those around us.

Furthermore, to uphold the validity of our relationship with Yahweh, we must be diligent in our pursuit of His guidance through prayer, study, and obedience. These practices serve as anchors that keep us grounded amidst life's storms. When we stand firm on Yahweh's promises, even amid trials and tribulations, our faith's validity is tested and proven. It becomes clear that our commitment is not based on falsehood but deeply rooted in the conviction that Yahweh is faithful and His Word is reliable.

Standing firm also entails resisting the temptation to conform to the temporary values of the age. It requires courage to declare openly that Yahweh's standards are what truly matter, regardless of the consequences. This steadfastness ensures that our lives remain effective and impactful. A faith that wavers or is compromised loses its potency. However, a faith that remains sincere and unchanging continues to bear fruit, bringing glory to Yahweh and blessing to others.

The efficacy of our faith hinges on this perseverance. When we remain valid, true to our convictions, and committed to Yahweh's truth, our lives become powerful testimonies of His grace. Our words and actions can inspire others to seek the same authentic relationship with the Creator Yahweh. In remaining steadfast, we mirror the steady nature of Yahweh Himself, whose promises are sure and whose love endures forever. The journey of faith is one of continuous choice, choosing daily to stand firm for Yahweh. It is about remaining valid and efficacious in our walk with Him, rooted in sincerity and unchangeable commitment.

As we do so, we not only preserve the integrity of our own spiritual lives but also become vessels through which Yahweh's truth and power are made manifest in the world. Let us therefore hold fast to this noble calling, confident that in remaining faithful, we participate in the divine assurance that Yahweh's Word and His promises are forever trustworthy and alive. In the journey of life, we are often met with hardships, setbacks, and moments of deep despair. It is during these times that our true character is revealed, and our capacity to endure is tested. To endure is to persevere through difficulties, to withstand the storms that threaten to overwhelm us, and to remain steadfast in our faith and beliefs. At the heart of enduring successfully lies a profound commitment which is a fight for Yahweh, our Creator and Sustainer.

Endurance is not merely about passive survival. It is an active, deliberate choice to continue fighting for what is right, trusting that the Lord Yahweh is with us through every trial. When we face suffering whether physical, emotional, or spiritual, we are called not to give up but to hold on, to seek strength in the Lord's Yahweh promises, and to press forward with steady hope. The Bible is full of stories of those who endured great suffering because they believed in Yahweh's sovereignty and goodness. Their stories serve as a testament that enduring is an act of faith, a fight for Yahweh's glory and for the fulfillment of His divine purpose in our lives.

Fighting for Yahweh means standing firm in our beliefs despite societal pressures, rejection, or persecution. It involves choosing to remain loyal to His laws, statues, judgements and commandments and trusting in His plan even when circumstances seem bleak. This fight is not a battle against people but a spiritual warfare, resisting doubt, fear, and temptation that seek to undermine our faith. It is a daily commitment to lean on Yahweh's strength and to remember that Yahweh is our refuge and fortress, a shelter in times of trouble. Enduring successfully requires a sincere heart, an honest acknowledgment of our weaknesses and a reliance on divine mercy. We must realize that our strength alone is low, but with Yahweh's power, we can overcome any obstacle. The scripture encourages us in, see Case Law § 2 Timothy 4:7: "I have fought a good fight, I have finished *my* course, I have kept the faith". This verse reminds us that enduring is a continual fight, a race we run with perseverance, holding tightly to our faith in Yahweh until the very end.

Furthermore, enduring for Yahweh is intertwined with hope. Hope sustains us when the road is long and the burden is heavy. It reassures us that our struggles are temporary and that Yahweh's promises are sure. As we fight to stay faithful, we anchor ourselves in His Word and prayer, drawing strength from His presence. We understand that our endurance is not in vain but is an essential part of our spiritual growth and sanctification. To endure successfully is also to trust that Yahweh's timing is perfect. Sometimes, we must wait patiently for Yahweh's deliverance, knowing that His plans are higher than ours. Waiting can be difficult, but faith teaches us to continue fighting in prayer, steadfast in our trust, until the Lord Yahweh answers in His perfect way and time.

To endure is to remain committed to fighting for Yahweh with sincerity and unchanging faith. It is a courageous act of loyalty that requires resilience, hope, and trust in His sovereignty. Through enduring, we testify to Yahweh's goodness and faithfulness, demonstrating that with Yahweh's strength, we can overcome every challenge. Let us remember that enduring is not just about surviving but about standing firm in our faith, fighting for Yahweh's glory, and finishing our race strong, trusting that our perseverance will ultimately lead us into the victorious presence of our Lord Yahweh. Courage is a profound and vital quality that sustains us through life's most challenging moments. It is not merely the absence of fear, but the ability to face our fears and difficulties with steady strength and resolve. To truly bear courage, we must learn to tolerate without flinching, standing firm in the face of adversity, pain, and uncertainty. Such resilience is rooted in a deep sense of trust and reliance on something greater than ourselves.

One of the most sincere and meaningful ways to cultivate this kind of courage is to ask Yahweh, our Creator and Source of all strength, for divine help. When we turn to Him in prayer, humbly acknowledging our limitations and weakness, we invite His power into our lives. It is through this heartfelt connection that we find the courage to endure hardships without shrinking back or giving in to fear.

To ask Yahweh for courage is to recognize that human strength alone is often inadequate. Life can present us with circumstances that threaten to overwhelm us like loss, failure, suffering, or the weight of responsibilities that seem too heavy to bear. In those moments, prayer becomes a vital act of surrender and trust. We can pray, sincerely and earnestly, asking Yahweh to fortify our hearts and give us the resilience to stand firm. This prayer is not a plea for ease or avoidance of difficulties, but a plea for the strength to face them with dignity and hope.

The Bible, a timeless source of knowledge and wisdom, offers numerous examples of individuals who demonstrated extraordinary courage through their faith in Yahweh. David, facing Goliath, did not rely on his own strength alone but trusted in Yahweh's power to deliver him. Esther risked her life to save her people, trusting in divine guidance. These stories remind us that true courage is rooted in faith and an unwavering belief that Yahweh is with us in every trial.

When we ask Yahweh for courage, we also commit ourselves to a sincere trust that He will equip us with what we need. Courage is not always the lack of fear. Often, it is the decision to move forward despite fear, trusting that Yahweh's presence and mercy will sustain us. This trust allows us to tolerate hardships without flinching, to bear suffering without losing hope, and to stand tall in the face of adversity. Furthermore, developing courage through prayer and faith helps us develop an adaptable spirit that can inspire others. Our willingness to face difficulties with bravery and perseverance can serve as a light of hope in our communities. It reminds those around us that, with Yahweh's help, we can endure and overcome even the most formidable obstacles.

True courage is a gift that can be obtained through sincere prayer and unchanging trust in Yahweh. Asking for Yahweh's strength is an act of humility and faith, opening the door for divine mercy to work within us. As we learn to tolerate without flinching and bearing our challenges with steadfastness, we grow in character and deepen our relationship with Yahweh. Let us always remember that with Yahweh by our side, we can face anything with courage, hope, and a resilient heart.

In the journey of life, we are continually called to make choices that define who we are and what we stand for. Among the most profound commitments we can make is the pledge of allegiance, not merely to a cause or a nation, but to the principles of righteousness, truth, and unchangeable devotion to Yahweh. This allegiance is not a temporary sentiment. It is a steadfast declaration to resist wickedness in all its forms, for ourselves, for our loved ones, and for the glory of our Creator Yahweh.

To truly pledge allegiance in this context means to establish a firm barrier against the encroachment of evil within our hearts and in the world around us. Wickedness seeks to deceive, to corrupt, and to enslave us into darkness. It whispers promises of pleasure, power, or convenience but ultimately leads to destruction. Resisting wickedness is not always easy. It requires courage, discipline, and a sincere commitment to uphold what is just and holy. We must remind ourselves that this resistance is not merely a defensive stance, but a proactive stand for righteousness to protect our souls, our families, and our communities from the snares of evil.

Our allegiance to Yahweh is the anchor that sustains this resistance. Yahweh is the embodiment of goodness, justice, mercy, and truth. To be loyal to Him is to align ourselves with His divine will, to reflect His character in our words and actions. In doing so, we declare that our primary allegiance is not to momentary worldly powers or personal desires, but to the everlasting King whose reign is righteous and whose ways are perfect. When we stand firm in our loyalty to Yahweh, we find the strength to oppose wickedness boldly, knowing that our efforts are rooted in divine authority and eternal truth.

This allegiance also calls us to resist wickedness for the sake of others. Our integrity and steadfastness can serve as a witness to those around us, inspiring others to also choose righteousness. When we resist evil, we become living testimonies of Yahweh's power to transform and sanctify. We demonstrate that it is possible to stand firm in the face of temptation and opposition, trusting that Yahweh's mercy is sufficient to empower us. Furthermore, this commitment necessitates humility and sincerity.

We must examine our own hearts, confess our shortcomings, and seek Yahweh's forgiveness and strength daily. Our resistance is not born out of arrogance or self-righteousness, but from a humble acknowledgment of our need for divine guidance and power. In our sincere allegiance to Yahweh, we find the motivation and decide to oppose wickedness not just outwardly, but within ourselves as well. Taking a stand of allegiance to Yahweh is a solemn and heartfelt choice to resist wickedness for ourselves and for Him. It is a declaration of loyalty that anchors us amidst the chaos and evil of the world. By steadfastly resisting what is wrong and embracing what is righteous, we honor our Creator Yahweh and fulfill our purpose as His faithful servants. Let us hold this allegiance firmly, knowing that in doing so, we participate in the divine victory of good over evil, light over darkness, and life over death. May our lives be a testament to unwavering fidelity to Yahweh, and may our resistance be a beacon of hope and righteousness in a troubled world. To stand for something is to embody a purpose greater than oneself, to be a symbol of hope, integrity, and righteousness in a world often clouded by uncertainty and chaos. It is an act of conviction, a declaration that we are committed to certain truths and principles that guide our lives and influence those around us. To stand for something is to be unwavering in our beliefs, to serve as a beacon for others seeking direction, and to uphold the values that foster love, justice, and compassion. At the core of this calling is a profound understanding of what it means to truly stand for good. For many, the foundation of this moral stance is rooted in faith and divine guidance. In particular, Yahweh, the Creator and Sustainer of life, desires us to stand firmly for goodness. Throughout sacred scriptures and spiritual teachings, it is made clear that we are called to be representatives of divine love, justice, and mercy. Yahweh's desire is not merely for us to acknowledge what is good in theory, but to actively embody goodness in our actions, words, and choices.

Standing for good, therefore, is not a passive endeavor. It requires deliberate effort, courage, and a sincere heart. It asks us to choose kindness over cruelty, integrity over dishonesty, forgiveness over resentment, and humility over pride. It challenges us to be different from the prevailing currents of selfishness and injustice. When we stand for good, we become a living testimony of divine values. We reflect Yahweh's character in a world that desperately needs light and love.

Furthermore, Yahweh's call for us to stand for good is intertwined with our responsibility to advocate for the vulnerable, to defend the oppressed, and to promote peace among all people. It is an active stance that demands vigilance and compassion. To stand for good is to refuse to turn a blind eye to evil and injustice. Instead, it is about courageously speaking out against wrong, offering help where suffering exists, and seeking reconciliation where division has taken root.

Sincerity lies at the heart of truly standing for good. It is not enough to perform acts of kindness out of obligation or for appearances. Genuine commitment requires a sincere love for others and a desire to see humanity flourish in truth and righteousness. When Yahweh calls us to stand for good, He is inviting us to internalize these values deeply, so they become part of who we are. This sincerity gives our actions authenticity and our words weight, making us true symbols of divine goodness.

In the long run, standing for good also means being patient and persistent. It is a journey filled with challenges and setbacks, but our steadfastness can inspire others and slowly transform communities. When we remain committed to what is right, even in the face of opposition, we honor Yahweh's desire for us to be symbols of unwavering hope and moral clarity. To stand for good is to accept a divine calling to be a living testament to righteousness and love. It is a sincere commitment to embody the principles Yahweh desires for us: kindness, justice, mercy, humility, and truth. As we do so, we become symbols of hope, a reflection of divine goodness that can inspire change, foster unity, and bring light into the darkness. Let us embrace this calling with sincerity and courage, knowing that in standing for good, we participate in the divine plan to make the world a better place.

In the quiet moments of life, when the world seems to weigh heavily upon your shoulders, it is easy to feel overwhelmed, to want to retreat, or to give in to the pressure of unrighteousness. Yet, true strength lies not in the absence of fear or hardship, but in the unchanging resolve to stand tall despite them. To stand tall is to embody courage, resilience, and integrity—especially when it is most difficult. Standing tall is a conscious choice.

It is a commitment to uphold what is right, even when it is inconvenient or unpopular. It is about refusing to back down in the face of injustice, oppression, or wrongdoing. When others compromise or turn away, the person who stands tall remains rooted in their principles, holding their ground with dignity. This kind of strength is not born out of arrogance or pride, but out of a sincere belief in truth and righteousness. The world often tests our resolve. It presents us with situations where unrighteousness is masked as power or where injustice appears to have the upper hand. It can be tempting to stay silent, to look the other way, or to take the easier path. But it is precisely in these moments that our true character is revealed. To stand tall means to recognize that the fight for justice is ongoing, and that giving in is never an option if we are to maintain our integrity. It means choosing to speak out against wrongs, to defend those who are vulnerable, and to act in accordance with our deepest values, regardless of the consequences. Courage is not the absence of fear. It is the willingness to face that fear with an open heart. Strength is not the absence of struggle. It is the perseverance to continue despite it. Calmness is not the absence of emotion, but a steady presence that anchors us amidst chaos. When we stand tall, we embody all of these qualities. We face adversity with a calm determination, knowing that our purpose is greater than any temporary setback. Standing tall requires inner strength and a conviction that goes beyond our outside circumstances. It involves remaining true to ourselves and to what we believe is right. It involves patience, resilience, and a deep-seated trust that justice, eventually, will prevail. It is easy to be swayed by intimidation or fear, but true courage is about maintaining our moral compass, even when the winds of opposition blow fiercely. To stand tall is also to be a beacon of hope and inspiration for others. When one person refuses to back down from unrighteousness, it ignites a ripple effect. It encourages those around us to find their own courage, to speak their truth, and to act with integrity. Our example can create change, however small, and remind the world that righteousness is worth fighting for.

In a world rife with challenges, setbacks, and injustices, remember this: Your strength, your courage, and your calmness are more powerful than any external force trying to silence or diminish you. Never underestimate the impact of standing firm in your values. Do not back down to unrighteousness. Instead stand tall, confident, compassionate, and unwavering, knowing that true power lies in the conviction to do what is right, even when it is hardest. Let your stance be a testament to the resilience of the human spirit. Let it be a reminder that, regardless of how dark the night may seem, the dawn begins with the courage to stand tall. For in standing tall, we not only define ourselves but also pave the way for others to follow, creating a world where righteousness and truth prevail. To serve as a sign or symbol of true devotion and steady faith, it is essential to understand what it means to represent, especially in the context of our relationship with Yahweh. To represent Yahweh wholeheartedly is to embody His virtues, His love, His justice, and His mercy in every aspect of our lives. It is a profound commitment to reflect His light and His truth, not just in words, but in actions, thoughts, and intentions.

Representing Yahweh wholeheartedly requires a sincere dedication that goes beyond fake gestures. It calls for a deep inner alignment with His teachings and a genuine desire to exemplify His character. When we seek to serve as a sign of Yahweh's presence, we become living symbols of His mercy and His sovereignty. Our lives should mirror His holiness, demonstrating humility, kindness, patience, and steady trust in His divine plan.

To truly represent Yahweh unequivocally is to recognize that our actions speak volumes about our faith. It means striving to act with integrity and love, even when it is challenging. It calls for a steadfast commitment to embody righteousness and to be a witness to His goodness in the world. When others see us, they should see not just a person, but a reflection of Yahweh's love and mercy, an outward sign pointing toward His greatness. This representation is not about perfection, but about sincerity and earnest effort. It's about living in a way that honors Yahweh, acknowledging His presence in every decision and interaction. Whether in moments of joy or times of trial, we are called to remain faithful, serving as a consistent and genuine sign of His everlasting contract.

Furthermore, representing Yahweh earnestly involves a willingness to serve others compassionately and selflessly. It is in our acts of kindness, our words of encouragement, and our willingness to forgive that His image is vividly displayed. We become symbols of His grandeur because we emulate His love, an unconditional, sacrificial love that seeks to uplift and bring hope. In essence, to represent Yahweh sincerely is to dedicate our entire being (heart, mind, body, and soul) to reflecting His divine nature. It is to understand that our lives are not our own, but are entrusted to us as a testament to His sovereignty. Our every act, every word, and every thought should aim to serve as a sign of His presence and power. Let us strive daily to be true representations of Yahweh, humble, sincere, and steadfast in our devotion. May our lives serve as enduring symbols of His love, guiding others toward His light and reminding all of His everlasting goodness. In doing so, we fulfill our highest calling to be living signs of Yahweh's presence in the world. In recent times, we have been witnesses to a world that often seems dominated by wrongs, corruption, and wickedness. It is with a sincere and heavy heart that I stand before you today to speak about the importance of protesting against such wicked rulership. Our voices are powerful tools, and when used rightly, they can serve as a beacon of hope and a call for change in the face of tyranny and moral decay.

Our world is cluttered with rulers who have lost their sense of responsibility, who govern not with the welfare of their people in mind but for personal gain, greed, and power. These leaders, instead of guiding with wisdom and compassion, often perpetrate wrongs, suppress dissent, and perpetuate suffering. Their wickedness undermines the very fabric of our societies, destroying trust, fostering inequality, and perpetuating cycles of despair. It is a moral imperative that we do not remain silent in the face of such corruption. Standing against wicked rulership is an act rooted in sincerity and genuine concern for the well-being of our communities and future generations. It is a way to stand up for what is right, to demand accountability, and to uphold the dignity of every individual who has been wronged or oppressed. When we stand up, we give voice to the voiceless, shine a light on darkness, and affirm that tyranny and injustice will not be tolerated. Our protests are not mere acts of rebellion. They are acts of moral courage and love for justice.

History has shown us time and time again that change often begins with a single step: an act of defiance, or a peaceful demonstration, or a collective voice rising against wrongdoing. Movements for civil rights, freedom, and equality have all started with protests. These acts of collective expression remind us that wicked rulers thrive in silence and secrecy, but when we come together publicly and peacefully to oppose their wickedness, we weaken their grip and pave the way for a better, more just society.

It is crucial that our objections are sincere and peaceful. Genuine protest stems from a desire for truth, justice, and the betterment of society. We must dispute not out of hatred or violence but out of love for our communities and a shared hope for a brighter future. Our voices should be tempered with compassion, our words with wisdom, and our actions with respect for human dignity. By doing so, we maintain the moral high ground and demonstrate that our cause is rooted in righteousness.

Objecting against wicked rulership is also a responsibility we owe to future generations. If we remain silent while injustice reigns, we betray not only ourselves but also the children who will inherit the world we leave behind. Our objections serve as a testament that we refused to accept evil as a norm and that we fought for a society where justice, equity, and morality prevail.

I urge each of you to consider the power of your voice and the importance of standing against wicked rulership. Our collective complaints which should be peaceful, sincere, and steady, can dismantle the walls of corruption and pave the way for a more just and compassionate world. Let us be courageous in our convictions, steadfast in our pursuit of justice, and sincere in our desire for a society where righteousness triumphs over wickedness. Together, through our conflicts, we can be the change we wish to see in the world.

Chapter 5

In a world often marked by brief shades of morality and the shifting sands of human virtue, there exists a standard, an ideal that transcends all earthly measures like the divine or the godlike. To aspire toward this is to seek the embodiment of qualities that echo the very essence of Yahweh, the eternal, the omniscient, and the omnipotent. Such qualities are not merely admirable. They are the highest form of existence, the purest expression of righteousness, and the ultimate goal of those who desire to live with integrity and purpose.

To be godlike is to accept only behaviors that reflect divine perfection. It requires a steadfast commitment to truth, a steady dedication to honesty that refuses to be swayed by deception, manipulation, or falsehood. The Divine is unchanging. It embodies truth in its purest form. In our lives, this means refusing to distort reality for personal gain or to mask our shortcomings behind lies. It involves a sincere acknowledgment of our faults and a sincere effort to grow beyond them, grounded in humility and a desire for genuine goodness. Tell the truth.

Furthermore, godlike behavior includes compassion and mercy. It demands that we see beyond ourselves, recognizing the inherent worth of every individual, regardless of their flaws or differences. To accept only godlike conduct is to embody unconditional love, offering forgiveness where it is due, extending mercy in moments of weakness, and acting with kindness that arises from a deep sense of empathy. Such compassion is not shallow but rooted in a profound understanding that all humans are imperfect beings deserving of dignity and respect.

Justice is another cornerstone of the godlike way of living. It calls for equity, integrity, and a refusal to accept wrongs in any form. To behave in a godlike manner means to stand for righteousness even when it is difficult, to uphold principles that promote equity and truth, and to act with unchanging dedication to the common good. It involves making sacrifices when necessary, not for personal glory, but because it is the right thing to do. This kind of justice requires a sincere heart that values moral consistency over convenience. Patience and humility are also essential qualities of Yahweh. They teach us to endure hardships without bitterness and to accept our limitations with virtue. To be godlike is to understand that perfection is a divine attribute, not a human one, and to recognize our dependence on divine guidance. It demands a sincere humility that recognizes our need for continual growth and an openness to correction and learning. Furthermore, accepting only godlike behavior means rejecting arrogance, pride, malice, and hatred which are behaviors that tarnish the soul and distance us from Yahweh. It means cultivating a spirit of humility that acknowledges our dependence on divine mercy and the interconnectedness of all creation. It involves a sincere desire to emulate divine qualities, not for personal elevation, but to reflect the divine glory that is beyond human comprehension. Living in such a manner is indeed challenging. It calls for persistent effort, sincere intention, and a humble recognition of our imperfections. Yet, it is also profoundly rewarding. By aligning ourselves with godlike qualities, we elevate our lives, fostering peace within and around us. We become reflections of divine goodness, a light in a world often shadowed by selfishness and despair. Ultimately, to accept only godlike behavior is to commit ourselves to a higher standard, one that resonates deeply with the core of what it means to be truly human. It is a pursuit rooted in sincere love for the divine, steadfast integrity, and an earnest desire to embody the best qualities that reflect the divine image within us. In doing so, we not only honor Yahweh but also forge a life of meaning, purpose, and authentic goodness thereby living truly as beings made in the image of Yahweh.

When we speak of something that is truly superb, we are touching upon a level of excellence that transcends ordinary understanding, a quality so profound that it resonates deeply within our souls. To perceive something as superb is to recognize an embodiment of perfection, a manifestation of divine brilliance that elevates the spirit and stirs the heart to reverence. And at the core of this perception lies an essence that exudes Yahweh's divine moral behavior attributes, which is an echo of the divine nature that infuses everything truly superb with its sanctity and majesty.

Yahweh, the Creator of all that exists, embodies qualities of immeasurable service, unwavering justice, boundless mercy, and infinite wisdom. When we encounter something superb, whether it be a masterpiece of artistry, a moment of profound truth, or an act of genuine kindness, we are, in a sense, glimpsing a reflection of His divine behavior. It is as if the very essence of Yahweh's love and righteousness flows through what is superb, illuminating it with a divine light that calls us to higher understanding and betterment.

To exude Yahweh's divine behavior is to demonstrate qualities that are rooted in humility, compassion, and integrity which are traits that elevate, sanctify, and inspire. True superbness operates not merely on the surface but emanates from a pure heart committed to truth and goodness. When we act with kindness, justice, and mercy, we mirror divine characteristics, and our actions become a testament to divine excellence. Such acts are not driven by superficial motives but grounded in a sincere desire to reflect the divine nature that Yahweh exemplifies for all humanity.

The concept of superbness infused with Yahweh's divine behavior invites us to see the sacred in the ordinary and the extraordinary alike. It beckons us to recognize that the truly superb is not just a matter of skill or achievement but a reflection of divine virtue. Whether it is in a work of art that stirs the soul, or a moment of genuine forgiveness, or a selfless act of service, each bears the mark of the Divine, exuding divine behavior that elevates human experience beyond the mundane and into the realm of the sacred.

Sincerity is essential in perceiving and embodying the superb. Genuine recognition of divine excellence requires an honest acknowledgment of our own limitations and a humble desire to grow closer to the divine qualities we admire. When we approach life with sincerity, our actions become authentic expressions of divine behavior. Our words and deeds cease to be superficial and instead reflect the divine love and wisdom that Yahweh exemplifies. Furthermore, embracing the divine nature in our pursuit of superbness encourages us to cultivate patience, humility, and steadfastness. Just as Yahweh's divine behavior is characterized by mercy and uniform justice, our efforts to embody these qualities must be sincere and persistent. True superbness is not temporary. It is rooted in a consistent dedication to embodying divine virtues, even amidst trials and challenges. It is in these moments that the divine within us is most vividly revealed.

In essence, the pursuit of the truly superb is a spiritual journey that calls us to align our actions, intentions, and hearts with the divine behavior exemplified by Yahweh. It is a call to be sincere in our desire to reflect divine goodness, recognizing that the highest form of excellence is that which exudes divine love, justice, and mercy. When we do so, we elevate not only ourselves but also inspire those around us to seek a higher standard or ideal where the Divine's presence is palpably felt in our everyday lives. To live and perceive in this manner is to recognize that the truly superb exists not merely in achievements or possessions but in the sacred qualities of the heart. It is to see the divine reflected in every act of goodness and to strive, with sincerity and humility, to mirror Yahweh's divine behavior in all that we do. In doing so, we partake in the sacred. We become vessels of divine excellence that exude beauty, truth, love, and supreme good in the purest sense of the word. Heaven is more than just a distant place we hope to reach someday. It is a state of being, a divine mindset that Yahweh desires for each of us to cultivate here on earth and beyond. When we think of heaven, many imagine pearly gates, streets of gold, and eternal bliss. While these images capture the beauty and majesty of the divine realm, the true essence of heaven is rooted in the heart, the mind, and in the state of soul that aligns with Yahweh's love, peace, and righteousness.

Yahweh, our Creator, longs for us to enter into a blessed state of mind characterized by trust, humility, gratitude, and a fixed faith. This heavenly mindset is not reserved solely for the afterlife. It is a gift and a calling that invites us to experience divine peace and joy in our daily lives. When our thoughts are centered on Yahweh's goodness and His promises, we begin to see the world through a lens of hope and divine purpose. In this way, heaven becomes a present reality, not just a future destination. The Bible often emphasizes that the kingdom of heaven is within us. Yahweh teaches us that the blessedness of heaven starts within our hearts, shaping how we perceive ourselves and others. The more we align our thoughts and actions with Yahweh's will, the closer we come to incorporate the heavenly nature. This alignment brings a sense of calm amid chaos, joy amid sorrow, and love amid division. It is a blessed state of mind that transcends circumstances, anchoring us in divine peace regardless of outward trials.

Yahweh desires that we think of ourselves as citizens of heaven, even while we walk this earth. Our mental and spiritual posture should reflect the eternal realities of Yahweh's kingdom like kindness, forgiveness, patience, humility, and compassion. When we nurture these qualities in our hearts, we mirror the divine goodness that makes heaven so radiant. Living with a heaven-focused mindset transforms our relationships and daily experiences, allowing us to serve others with genuine love and to find contentment in even the simplest blessings.

To cultivate this blessed state of mind, we must intentionally turn our thoughts toward Yahweh through prayer, meditation on His Word, and conscious gratitude. It requires surrendering worries and burdens, trusting in His sovereignty and goodness. As we do so, our hearts become more aligned with heaven's harmony. We begin to see beyond temporary troubles, recognizing instead the eternal hope and divine privilege that sustains us.

Heaven, then, is not just a future promise but a present reality that begins within us. Yahweh wants us to live in a perpetual state of blessedness rooted in His love and characterized by inner peace and joy. This heavenly mindset transforms our outlook on life, our interactions with others, and our approach to each day. It invites us to walk in a manner worthy of our heavenly calling, to carry the peace of heaven wherever we go, and to reflect the glory of Yahweh in all that we do.

In embracing this divine perspective, we become more than just followers of faith. We become living testimonies of the kingdom of heaven. We embody the blessedness that Yahweh desires for us such as being peaceful, joyful, and in harmony with His divine purpose. This is the blessed state of heaven that our Creator longs for us to experience now, a taste of eternal life that begins in the heart and overflows into every aspect of our existence.

May we strive to nurture this heavenly mindset each day, trusting in Yahweh's love and mercy. May our thoughts be anchored in His promises, our spirits lifted by His presence, and our lives a reflection of the blessedness that heaven offers. Because in doing so, we draw nearer to the divine reality, the blessed eternal state of heaven that Yahweh has prepared for those who love Him. When we consider the concept of "first class," our minds often turn to luxurious comfort, superior service, and a sense of elite distinction. However, beyond the realm of travel and luxury, the idea of "first class" can take on a deeper, more meaningful significance. It can symbolize excellence, primacy, and the highest standard of importance. In this context, when we speak of something being "of or relating to first class," we are referring to its paramount status, its unmatched quality, and its central place of honor.

In a spiritual sense, the notion of "first class" extends beyond material wealth or social status. It touches on the very foundation of our values and beliefs. At the heart of many faiths and spiritual teachings is the recognition of what holds the highest priority or what is truly first in our lives. For those who believe in the divine, this "first class" status is often reserved for Yahweh, the Supreme Being, the Creator of all that exists. Yahweh, in the Hebrew tradition, is acknowledged as first class in the grand hierarchy of existence. This is not merely a designation of importance but an affirmation of His primacy over all creation. He is the Alpha and the Omega, the beginning and the end, signifying that everything else flows from Him and ultimately finds its purpose in Him. To say that Yahweh is first class is to acknowledge that He is the ultimate source of life, truth, love, and justice. No other entity or pursuit can truly occupy the highest position unless it is aligned with His divine will.

Recognizing Yahweh as first class requires sincerity and humility. It is an honest acknowledgment that His greatness surpasses all human understanding, and His authority is unmatched. It calls for placing Him at the very center of our lives, prioritizing our relationship with Him above all else. This is not a mere random label but a heartfelt commitment to honor His supremacy through our actions, thoughts, and intentions.

The sincerity of this recognition stems from an understanding that Yahweh's first class status is rooted in His unending goodness and mercy. His love is fixed, His justice is perfect, and His sovereignty is absolute. When we embrace Yahweh as the first in our lives, we embrace the very foundation of true fulfillment and purpose. It is in putting Him first that we find stability, peace, and direction amid life's uncertainties.

Furthermore, acknowledging Yahweh as first class encourages us to reflect on our own priorities. Are we living in a way that honors His supremacy? Do we seek to serve Him with genuine sincerity, or are we distracted by short-term worldly pursuits? The journey towards placing Yahweh in the first class seat of our hearts is one of continual self-examination and dedication. It involves cultivating a sincere love for Him, trusting in His plan, and striving to match His virtues.

When we speak of first class, we can extend that admiration and respect into the spiritual realm by recognizing Yahweh's supreme status. He is the first and the foremost, the one who deserves our highest praise and devotion. Sincerely acknowledging that Yahweh is first class in our lives transforms our perspective, enriching our faith and guiding us toward a life of genuine purpose and divine alignment. It is a heartfelt journey to honor the one who is truly first in all things, a journey that elevates our souls and deepens our understanding of what it means to live in genuine truth and love. Excellence is a pursuit that transcends mere achievement or superficial success. It is an enduring commitment to being, doing, and manifesting the very best within us. To be "very good of its kind," or eminently good, is not simply about reaching a certain standard but about expressing a higher principle or a standard rooted in integrity, virtue, and a genuine desire to reflect the divine qualities bestowed upon us.

At the heart of this pursuit of excellence lies a profound truth: Yahweh, our Creator, desires us to be superior in character. This is not a call to arrogance or pride but a sacred invitation to develop virtues that mirror His goodness. In the scriptures, we are often reminded that Yahweh values the inward qualities of the heart such as kindness, patience, humility, and love that define us far more than external accomplishments. Our character, therefore, becomes the foundation upon which excellence is built. See Case Law § **1 Samuel 16:7.**

Yahweh's desire for us to be superior in character is an expression of His love and His vision for us as His children. He wants us to rise above mediocrity, to strive for moral and spiritual heights that reflect His own holiness. This superiority is not about surpassing others in a competitive sense but about surpassing our former selves, continuously growing in integrity, wisdom, compassion, and humility. When we cultivate these qualities, we align ourselves with divine excellence, a standard that is pure, unfailing, and inspiring.

The journey toward excellence rooted in divine character is never easy. It requires honest self-examination, discipline, and a sincere desire to grow beyond our shortcomings. It means choosing patience over impatience, humility over pride, forgiveness over resentment. It involves a conscious effort to live out virtues in our daily interactions, to treat others with respect and kindness, and to hold ourselves accountable to higher standards. Such a life is not marked by perfection but by persistent effort and humility in the pursuit of becoming better. Moreover, genuine excellence is characterized by consistency. It's about showing up each day with a heart committed to goodness, even when no one is watching. It's about doing what is right because it is right, not because it is easy or advantageous. In this way, our character becomes a testament to our faith and our desire to imitate divine qualities. The pursuit of excellence in character is also deeply intertwined with purpose. Recognizing that Yahweh wants us to be superior in character, gives our efforts a divine purpose that transcends personal success and aims at glorifying Him through our conduct. When our lives reflect virtues such as honesty, humility, service, and love, we become living testimonies to His goodness. Our excellence then becomes a light that draws others toward divine truth and inspires them to pursue similar heights of character.

In the end, the very essence of true excellence is found in humility, a recognition that we are always a work in progress, continuously being shaped by divine mercy. We must acknowledge that our strength and capacity for goodness come from Yahweh Himself. As we seek to be eminently good, we open ourselves to His transforming power, allowing His Spirit to cultivate in us the qualities that reflect His character. To be very good of its kind or eminently good is a noble and worthy aspiration. It is an expression of sincere devotion to becoming more like Yahweh, illustrating His virtues, and striving for a life that is not just successful in worldly terms but profoundly good in character. Such excellence is the highest form of living, a reflection of divine love and goodness in every thought, word, and deed. It is a lifelong journey, but one that leads us closer to the divine purpose for which we were created. We become beings of true excellence or eminently good in the sight of our Creator. Justice is more than just a societal ideal. It is a fundamental reflection of moral uprightness and goodness. To act justly means to act in accordance with what is morally right, just, and equitable. It is an enduring virtue that guides our interactions, decisions, and intentions, ensuring that we uphold the dignity and rights of others. Throughout history and across cultures, justice has been recognized as a cornerstone of a righteous life, and for those who believe in Yahweh, it holds an even deeper significance. Yahweh, the Creator of all, desires that His followers carry out just measures in every aspect of their lives. This divine expectation is clear in many scriptures, where justice is not merely recommended but commanded. For instance, in the Torah, Yahweh emphasizes the importance of justice multiple times. See Case Law **§ Leviticus 19:15** states, "Ye shall do no unrighteousness in judgment: thou shalt not respect the person of the poor, nor honour the person of the mighty: *but* in righteousness shalt thou judge thy neighbour." Such directives reveal that Yahweh's standard for justice is thorough and impartial, rooted in righteousness and truth. Living justly means more than simply avoiding wrongdoing; it involves actively pursuing open-mindedness and equity in our dealings with others. It requires us to be honest, to treat people with respect and compassion, and to stand against wrongs wherever we see it. Yahweh's desire is that His people reflect His own character like that of righteousness, mercy, and love through our actions. When we carry out just measures, we honor His commandments and demonstrate our commitment to His moral standards.

Furthermore, Yahweh's call for justice is intertwined with His love for the oppressed and needy. Throughout Scripture, we see His concern for the vulnerable and His condemnation of exploitation, corruption, and unjust treatment. See Case Law **§ Isaiah 1:17** urges us to "Learn to do well; seek judgment, relieve the oppressed, judge the fatherless, plead for the widow." These words remind us that justice is not passive but active; it calls us to advocate for those who cannot defend themselves and to ensure equity in all circumstances.

In our daily lives, acting justly can manifest in many ways like being honest in our business dealings, speaking out against inequity, forgiving those who have wronged us, and making decisions that benefit the common good. It also involves humility and a recognition that our own understanding of what is just may be limited, calling us to seek divine guidance and wisdom in our judgments. Yahweh wants us to be diligent in measuring our actions against His standards, ensuring that our conduct aligns with what is morally good and upright.

Moreover, justice is a reflection of our love for Yahweh and for our neighbors. Yahshua summarized the law with two great commandments: "Thou shalt love the Lord Yahweh thy God with all thy heart, and with all thy soul, and with all thy mind", see Case Law **§ Matthew 22:37**. Justice is the practical expression of this love, treating others with equity and kindness because they are creations of Yahweh, deserving of dignity and respect.

Living in harmony with what is morally upright also involves repentance and humility. When we fall short of justice, Yahweh's mercy is available to us through repentance. He desires us to continually seek His guidance, to learn from our mistakes, and to grow in righteousness. By doing so, we become more faithful to His call for justice and righteousness. The pursuit of justice is an essential aspect of living a life that is sincere and aligned with Yahweh's will. It is His desire that we carry out just measures in all our dealings, representing His character in the world.

As we strive to act justly whether in our personal relationships, our communities, or in societal structures, we honor His commandments and manifest His kingdom on earth. Let us remember that justice is not merely a duty but a reflection of our love for Yahweh and our commitment to doing what is morally good. May we seek His wisdom diligently and live out justice in all that we do, so that our lives may be pleasing in His sight and His righteousness may shine through us. The concept of what is proper is fundamentally rooted in the idea of being suitable, right, and appropriate in a given situation. At its core, being proper goes beyond mere surface appearances or societal expectations. It contains a profound sense of moral fitness and alignment with what is right in the eyes of Yahweh. To truly understand what it means to be proper, one must consider the standards set forth by divine guidance and recognize that true propriety is rooted in moral integrity and righteousness. In our daily lives, we often strive to present ourselves in ways that are deemed suitable or appropriate whether in our language, actions, or attitudes. However, genuine propriety requires more than shallow correctness. It calls us to evaluate our inner motives and to ensure that our behavior reflects a heart aligned with divine principles. Being proper in Yahweh's sight involves a sincere effort to live with moral fitness, demonstrating honesty, kindness, humility, and love. It is about doing what is right not just outwardly, but inwardly, knowing that Yahweh judges the heart as well as the actions. Morally fit individuals in Yahweh's eyes are those who seek to promote virtues that honor Him. This means avoiding behaviors that are dishonest, unjust, or harmful, and instead embracing integrity, justice, compassion, and humility. Such moral fitness is not achieved through mere rule-following but through a genuine change of the heart. When our desires and actions align with Yahweh's moral standards, our conduct naturally becomes proper or appropriate in the highest sense because it reflects His righteousness. Furthermore, being proper in Yahweh's view requires humility and a recognition that our righteousness is dependent on His mercy. No amount of personal effort can fully attain moral perfection, but a sincere desire to please Him and live rightly is what makes our efforts proper. This sincerity is essential. It is not enough to perform outwardly correct actions while harboring inner selfishness or hypocrisy. True decorum involves authenticity, the kind of conduct that flows from a heart committed to honoring Yahweh.

In practical terms, living properly means integrating the love and humility exemplified by Yahweh's Son, Yahweh Ben Yahweh. It means treating others with respect and dignity, forgiving where forgiveness is due, and standing up for justice and righteousness. When our behavior consistently reflects these virtues, we demonstrate that we are morally fit and that our lives are aligned with divine standards. This alignment is what makes our conduct appropriate and right in Yahweh's eyes.

Ultimately, the pursuit of proper living is a journey of continuous growth and earnest effort. It is about aligning our will with Yahweh's will, seeking to be morally upright not just in appearance but in substance. When our hearts are sincere and our conduct is guided by a desire to please Yahweh, we can be confident that we are living properly or truly suitable, right, and appropriate in His sight. Such a life honors Him, fulfills His purpose for us, and reflects His glory to the world around us. In a world that often celebrates grandeur, achievement, and the relentless pursuit of more, the virtue of modesty stands as a quiet reminder of humility and sincerity. To be modest in thought and act is to adopt a way of life rooted in authenticity, humility, and a deep awareness of one's place within the larger tapestry of creation. It is an attitude that does not seek to elevate oneself above others but instead values the inherent dignity of every individual, recognizing that true worth is not measured by outward accomplishments or possessions but by the purity of one's heart and mind.

At the core of modesty lies an understanding that life is a gift from Yahweh, the Creator of all. In scripture, Yahweh often promotes behaviors that reflect humility and restraint, encouraging His followers to seek righteousness without arrogance. Modesty, therefore, is not merely about outward appearance or shallow humility. It is a reflection of inner purity or a sincere effort to align one's thoughts and actions with divine principles. When one is modest, they acknowledge that all good things come from Yahweh, and that human efforts are but a small part of His greater plan.

In the context of behavior, modesty manifests as a gentle strength or an ability to pursue goals and dreams without the arrogance of superiority or the temptation to chase after worldly accolades. Yahweh promotes "chase behavior," not in the sense of reckless pursuit of material success, but as a sincere longing for spiritual growth, righteousness, and service. To chase after righteousness with humility means to pursue one's purpose in life with an open heart, free from pride or envy. It is to seek truth and goodness diligently, yet quietly, trusting that Yahweh's timing and wisdom will guide the way. This pursuit requires a pure mind and a humble spirit which are qualities that keep one grounded even amidst achievement. Modesty in thought prevents one from becoming consumed by ego or vanity, reminding us that true fulfillment comes from aligning our desires with divine will rather than fleeting worldly desires. In our acts, modesty translates into sincerity and authenticity in doing good not for recognition, but because it is the right thing to do. It involves serving others with genuine compassion and humility, recognizing the divine image within each person. Living modestly also entails a recognition of limitations, an acknowledgment of dependence on Yahweh's mercy. It is an honest appraisal of one's abilities and achievements, never allowing pride to insulate us from humility or from the acknowledgment that all blessings come from Yahweh. This attitude fosters a life of integrity, meaning it is pure in thought and act, where intentions are sincere, and actions are guided by love and humility. Furthermore, Yahweh's promotion of chase behavior underscores the importance of perseverance and earnestness in our pursuits, yet always tempered by modesty. The genuine chase for righteousness involves patience, humility, and trust in divine timing. It encourages believers to be diligent without arrogance, ambitious without greed, and sincere without pretense. To be modest in thought and act, inspired by Yahweh's teachings and the divine promotion of chase behavior, is to live a life of authenticity and humility. It is to pursue our goals with a sincere heart, unwavering in faith, trusting in divine guidance, and always mindful of our place within Yahweh's creation. Such a life is not the path of superficial humility or empty modesty, but a profound, heartfelt commitment to embodying purity, sincerity, and humility in every thought and every action. It is through this modest pursuit that we draw closer to Yahweh and reflect His divine nature in our everyday lives.

In a world filled with distractions, temptations, and the constant pull of worldly desires, the desire to be free from fault remains a noble and essential pursuit. To be truly spotless is not merely about outward appearances or superficial cleanliness. It is about cultivating purity within our hearts, minds, bodies, and souls as well as aligning ourselves with the moral standards that Yahweh, our Creator, sets forth for us. This pursuit of holiness is a sincere journey, rooted in humility, devotion, and a deep longing to reflect His divine goodness. Yahweh looks beyond the outward and examines the heart. See Case Law **§ Proverbs 20:9** asks, "Who can say, 'I have kept my heart pure; I am clean and without sin'?". This question reminds us that true morality begins from within. Our hearts are the wellspring of our thoughts, intentions, and motives. If our hearts are stained with bitterness, envy, or selfishness, those impurities will inevitably seep into our actions and words. Therefore, maintaining a clean heart is foundational to living a life that is pleasing to Yahweh.

We are called to guard our hearts diligently, to meditate on what is true, noble, right, pure, lovely, and admirable. See Case Law **§ Philippians 4:8**. By filling our minds with healthy thoughts and turning away from harmful influences, we foster an environment within ourselves that is conducive to moral integrity. The battle for morality begins in the mind, and it requires constant vigilance and prayer. Yahweh's moral behavioral attributes are clear and high. His commandments serve as a blueprint for living a life that is not only free from sin but also a testament to His holiness working within us. To be morally upright means to act with integrity, compassion, and honesty. It involves resisting temptation, choosing righteousness over unrighteousness, and being accountable for our actions. Living according to Yahweh's moral principles demonstrates our sincere desire to be close to Him. It's a reflection of our respect for His holiness and our understanding that our conduct affects not only ourselves but also those around us. When we strive for moral behavior, we affirm our commitment to virtuousness and become vessels of His love and righteousness.

Virtue extends beyond the spiritual and moral to the physical. Our bodies are temples of the Holy Spirit, see Case Law **§1 Corinthians 6:19-20,** and as such, we should honor and care for them. This means avoiding practices and substances that defile or harm us, maintaining health, and practicing moderation. Physical cleanliness is a visible expression of our inner devotion and respect for Yahweh's creation. Equally important is the cleansing of our souls or our innermost selves. Daily repentance, prayer, and reflection are vital in removing the stains of guilt, shame, and sin. Through sincere repentance, we acknowledge our shortcomings and seek Yahweh's forgiveness, trusting in His promise to cleanse us from all unrighteousness. See Case Law **§ 1 John 1:9**. It is through these spiritual practices that our souls remain pure, vibrant, and aligned with His divine will. In the quiet moments of reflection, when we pause to consider the essence of our character and the depths of our intentions, we come face to face with a profound desire to be pure. To be pure is to be free from moral fault or guilt, an aspiration that echoes deeply within the human heart. It is an honorable pursuit, one that exceeds mere actions and touches the very core of our being.

Yahweh, in His infinite wisdom and love, desires for us not only to follow His commandments outwardly but to cultivate chasity within. He yearns for our hearts to be cleansed from the stain of selfishness, pride, and fault. When He calls us to be pure in heart and deeds, He is inviting us into a sacred journey—a journey toward sanctity, integrity, and genuine righteousness. This purity is not a superficial veneer but a sincere shift that manifests in our every thought, word, and action.

The Lord's Yahweh standard of goodness is rooted in His holiness. He is perfectly pure, and His desire is that His children imitate that holiness. To be pure in heart means to have an undivided devotion to Him, to love what He loves, and to eschew what is contrary to His will. It involves a sincere longing to reflect His goodness and to live in harmony with His principles. When our hearts are clean, our motives are sincere, and our intentions are aligned with divine truth. Such purity shields us from guilt because it stems from a genuine desire to please Yahweh, not merely to appear righteous in the eyes of others.

Furthermore, Yahweh calls us to be honest in our deeds. Our actions should be a reflection of the virtue that resides within us. When we act with integrity, kindness, honesty, and humility, we demonstrate that our hearts are genuinely aligned with Yahweh's will. A pure life is characterized by consistency or by the habit of making sure that what we do outwardly matches what we possess inwardly. It is a life free from deceptiveness, hypocrisy, and moral compromise. Living in this way, we find ourselves liberated from guilt because our conscience bears witness to our sincere commitment to righteousness.

This pursuit of righteousness is a continuous process. It requires humility, self-awareness, and a willingness to repent and be renewed daily. We are all imperfect, prone to stumble and fall, but Yahweh's mercy is abundant. When we stumble, genuine repentance restores our goodness, and we are once again able to stand before Him with a clear conscience. The key is to keep our hearts vigilant, guard our thoughts, and seek His guidance in every step we take.

Choosing to pursue righteousness in heart and deeds is ultimately an act of trust. So, trust that Yahweh's ways are best, trust that His mercy can purge even the most stained soul, and trust that living in righteousness is the path to true freedom. When we align ourselves with His divine standards, we are not only free from moral fault or guilt but also empowered to live lives that honor Him and reflect His divine nature. In this sincere pursuit, we find peace that comes from knowing we are walking in Yahweh's light, striving to be as pure as He is. And in this purity, we fulfill the divine calling to be His children, set apart and chosen to bear witness to His goodness in a world that desperately needs His love. May our hearts remain steadfast in this pursuit, seeking to be pure in all our ways, for in doing so, we mirror the holiness of Yahweh Himself and walk confidently in the path of righteousness. In our journey through life, we often encounter the challenge of maintaining integrity and chasity amidst a world that is frequently marred by corruption, deceit, and moral compromise. True cleanliness whether ceremonial, spiritual, or moral, goes beyond superficial appearances. It is a state of being that reflects inner virtue, a conscious effort to rid ourselves of everything that defiles our soul and separates us from the divine presence of Yahweh.

Yahweh, the Creator of all, is a God of perfect holiness and righteousness. His standards are unwavering, and He requires that His people approach Him without blemish or defect. The scriptures remind us time and again: "Yahweh will not accept blemishes", see Case Law **§ Leviticus 22:20-25**. This means that in our offerings, in our service, and in our lives, we are called to present ourselves as pure and unblemished or free from moral corruption, sinister connections, and any form of compromise that tarnishes our character.

To be truly clean is to dedicate ourselves wholeheartedly to righteousness. It involves a conscious effort to observe the rules of divine justice and moral uprightness. This means not just adhering to external laws, but also cultivating a heart that despairs of evil and seeks goodness. It is about cleansing our conscience from guilt and shame and renewing our commitment to walk in truth and honesty. When we align ourselves with Yahweh's standards, our lives become a testament to His holiness.

Ceremonial and spiritual cleanliness are deeply interconnected. They remind us that righteousness is not merely outward appearance but an inward state of the soul. Rituals and practices serve as symbols and reminders of our need for cleansing, but genuine purity comes from a sincere desire to be free from all moral corruption. We are to observe the commandments diligently, ensuring that our actions, thoughts, and motives are pure. Any sinister connection whether it be greed, envy, deception, or risk, defiles us and distances us from the divine favor we seek. The path to spiritual cleanliness requires preparation. We must constantly examine ourselves and be willing to succumb to any hidden sin or allegiance to darkness. This involves repentance, humility, and a genuine desire to be made whole. It also means surrounding ourselves with principles and relationships that promote righteousness and discourage evil influences.

Furthermore, true cleanliness is a gift from Yahweh, but it requires our active participation. We must seek His cleansing through prayer, confession, and obedience. When we come before Him with a contrite heart, acknowledging our faults and asking for His grace, we open ourselves to His transformative power.

His Spirit works within us to renew our minds, cleanse our hearts, and set us free from the moral and spiritual corruption that seeks to entangle us.

Remember, Yahweh's acceptance is reserved for those who are unblemished in spirit and truth. He is not pleased with offerings or sacrifices that are tainted by sin or moral compromise. Our lives should be a living sacrifice which means clean, pure, and dedicated to His glory. The essence of true worship involves presenting ourselves without blemish and ensuring that our hearts are aligned with His righteousness.

The journey toward being truly clean, whether ceremonially, spiritually, or morally, is a continuous one. It demands sincerity, discipline, and a heartfelt commitment to live according to Yahweh's standards. By rejecting corruption, observing His rules diligently, and sanctifying ourselves from all sinister attachments, we become vessels suitable for His use. Let us strive to be unblemished in His sight, for only then can we truly stand justified before Him and enjoy the fullness of His blessing. May we continually seek His face to cleanse our hearts, renew our spirits, and walk in the light of His holiness. For in living a life free from blemish, we honor Yahweh and reflect His divine righteousness to the world around us.

Chapter 6

Throughout human history, the question of morality has been a big concern for philosophers, theologians, and thinkers alike. What is right? What is wrong? And where do these distinctions originate? These questions become even more complex when we consider the nature of creation itself and the role of divine authority in shaping the moral landscape.

One perspective that challenges traditional notions of morality is the belief that the divine, specifically Yahweh, created both good and bad. This viewpoint suggests that what we often deem as immoral like acts of cruelty, deception, greed, or violence, are not merely human failings but are part of a larger, divine design. If Yahweh, as the ultimate creator, fashioned all aspects of existence, then the presence of what we perceive as evil or immoral could be understood as an intentional component of creation.

This idea causes us to reflect deeply on the nature of morality and immorality. Traditional morality often paints a clear paradox: good versus evil, right versus wrong. Yet, if the divine is responsible for creating all facets of reality, then the lines between these categories become blurred. Perhaps, in some sense, immorality is not simply an anomaly or a deviation from an ideal but is woven into the fabric of existence itself. The notion that Yahweh created bad challenges the simplistic view of divine goodness as the sole origin of morality. Instead, it invites us to consider that the Divine might include a spectrum of attributes where some are benevolent, and others are seemingly malevolent from our limited human viewpoint. This outlook can be unsettling, for it confronts us with the uncomfortable possibility that what we label as immoral serves a purpose within a grander cosmic order.

From this angle, acts traditionally considered immoral such as betrayal, cruelty, or selfishness, may have a role in the unfolding of life and evolution. They could serve as lessons, catalysts for growth, or necessary counterbalances to goodness. The existence of bad or immoral acts might be integral to free will, allowing humans to choose, to develop moral character, and to learn from their experiences.

In acknowledging that Yahweh created bad, we also confront the moral complexity within ourselves. Human beings, created by this divine force, carry within them the potential for both goodness and immorality. Recognizing that immorality may be part of the divine design does not absolve individuals of responsibility; rather, it challenges us to understand the deeper purpose behind our actions and the nature of the universe.

This outlook calls for humility and a sincere examination of our values. It urges us to question whether our moral judgments are absolute or if they are influenced by limited human understanding. If the divine include both good and bad, then the moral landscape is far richer and more intricate than simple black-and-white distinctions.

Ultimately, contemplating the idea that Yahweh created bad invites us into a profound reflection on the nature of morality itself. It beckons us to accept the complexity of divine creation and to acknowledge that what we perceive as immoral may have a place within a larger, perhaps incomprehensible, divine plan. Such a point of view fosters humility, compassion, and a sincere pursuit of understanding in our ongoing journey through life's moral labyrinth. In the quiet corners of history and the bustling streets of modern cities alike, one truth remains unwavering. Vice, moral depravity, and corruption are a silent insidious force that steadily erodes the foundation of any nation. It begins subtly, often unnoticed at first, but its corrosive effects are profound and far-reaching, eventually tearing apart the very fabric that holds a society together.

Wickedness, when left unchecked, promotes a culture of greed, dishonesty, and selfishness. Leaders driven by personal gain prioritize their own interests over the well-being of their people, betraying the trust placed in them. This moral decay seeps into institutions involving judicial practices, law enforcement, and education which corrupts their character and renders them ineffective. When those in power become entangled in vice, the moral compass of a nation spirals into chaos, and the rule of law becomes a mere illusion. The destructive power of sin is vividly evident in the decline of moral standards among ordinary citizens. As corruption becomes widespread, honesty is replaced by deceit, respect for others diminishes, and the sense of community erodes. People begin to see greed as a virtue, and morality as a hindrance to personal success. Such attitudes produce social division, weaken neighborly unity, and create an environment where crime and injustice flourish. The moral fabric of society becomes frayed and the trust, which was once the glue that holds communities together disintegrates.

Economically, corruption raises instability. When corruption corrupts financial systems, trade, and governance, it hinders just competition and discourages investment. Resources are siphoned off by those with power and influence, leaving the common people impoverished and disenfranchised. Over time, this economic decay fuels social unrest and political instability, pushing a nation toward chaos and decline.

The spiritual and cultural vitality of a nation also suffers under the weight of wickedness. Moral depravity often leads to a decline in values, respect for rule, and spiritual integrity. When selfishness and greed dominate, virtues such as compassion, humility, and decorum are cast aside. This spiritual rot destroys the moral backbone of society, leading to a sense of despair, hopelessness, and a loss of purpose among its people. History provides countless examples of civilizations that have fallen because of their own moral decline. Empires, once mighty and revered, crumbled under the weight of corruption and sin. Their leaders, blinded by greed and power, betrayed their people and abandoned their moral duties. The societal decay that followed was swift and irreversible, illustrating that no amount of military might or technological advancement can save a nation that has lost its moral compass.

To safeguard a nation's future, there must be a collective acknowledgment of the destructive nature of immorality. Moral etiquette, honesty, humility, and a genuine concern for the common good are the pillars that uphold a healthy society. Leaders must lead by example, advocating transparency and justice. Citizens must remain vigilant against corruption in all its forms, cultivating virtues that strengthen community bonds and promote genuine well-being. Wickedness is not merely a personal failing. It is a societal cancer that, if left unchecked, destroys the very soul of a nation. It corrupts individuals, demolishes institutions, and fractures social cohesion. The path to national decline is paved with moral depravity, and only through sincere commitment to virtue and rightness can a nation hope to survive and thrive. Let us remember that a society built on righteousness and virtue is resilient, enduring, and capable of achieving greatness, whereas one consumed by sin is doomed to decay. Throughout our lives, we all carry with us certain quirks and imperfections that linger beneath our outward appearance of stability and strength. These habitual and usually minor defects, known as foibles, are an intrinsic part of being human. They are the subtle, sometimes amusing, sometimes frustrating, manifestations of our imperfect nature. Yet, amidst these imperfections, there is a profound truth: Yahweh knows our shortcomings intimately. A flaw might be something as simple as misplacing keys, a tendency to speak too quickly, or a habit of biting one's nails when anxious. These are the little quirks that do not define us entirely but are part of the tapestry of our character. They often go unnoticed by others, or perhaps only noticed with a gentle smile or a shake of the head, yet they are ever-present. These small flaws can sometimes cause us embarrassment or shame, especially when we realize how often they appear in moments of vulnerability. But in light of divine understanding, they are viewed differently. Yahweh, in His infinite wisdom and compassion, is fully aware of every shortcoming, no matter how tiny it may seem to us. There is no flaw too small or too insignificant to escape His notice. This knowledge is not a source of judgment or condemnation but rather a testament to His intimate understanding of us. It reassures us that we are seen completely in our strengths and our imperfections alike. When we stumble in our daily routines, forget kindness in moments of stress, or cling stubbornly to our habits, we can rest assured that Yahweh perceives these moments with patience and love.

Understanding that Yahweh knows our shortcomings invites us to approach ourselves with gentleness and humility. Let us be reminded that perfection is not the only requirement. Rather, sincerity and a willingness to grow are what matters most. See Case Law **§ Matthew 5:48** KJV. Our faults do not disqualify us from divine favor. Instead, they serve as gentle reminders of our humanness and the ongoing process of spiritual and personal growth. They teach us patience both with ourselves and with others, and promote a sense of humility, knowing that we are all imperfect beings in need of divine mercy.

Recognizing our shortcomings also opens the door to humility in our relationships with others. When we understand that everyone carries their own faults, some visible, some hidden we can approach them with greater compassion and understanding. We are all, in some way, flawed and in need of mercy. This awareness can soften our judgments and help us extend kindness, patience, and forgiveness to those around us.

Moreover, knowing that Yahweh is aware of our weaknesses encourages us to seek His strength rather than relying solely on our own efforts. It is through divine favor that we find the power to overcome or accept our imperfections. We are invited to bring our flawed selves before Him, confident that His love is unwavering and complete. Our faults, no matter how small, become opportunities for humility and reliance on divine mercy.

In the end, our faults are a testament to our humanity. They are part of what makes us unique, real, and relatable. Yahweh's knowledge of our shortcomings reassures us that we are not alone in our imperfections. His love encompasses every flaw, every weakness, and every trivial defect. As we strive to grow and improve, let us remember that divine understanding is always present and ready to embrace us completely just as we are. In this awareness, we find comfort, hope, and the courage to persevere, knowing that we are continually held in love by the One who knows us fully.

Lowness, the quality or state of being weak, is a condition that many of us experience at different points in our lives. It manifests in moments when our strength falters, our confidence wanes, and we feel vulnerable or overwhelmed. In a world that often values strength, resilience, and independence, acknowledging and understanding lowness can be difficult. Yet, it is an inevitable part of the human experience, reminding us of our limitations and opening the door for growth, humility, and reliance on something greater.

Throughout our lives, we may face circumstances that leave us feeling physically, emotionally, or spiritually drained. Perhaps it is a season of hardship, loss, or failure that strips us of our perceived strength. In these moments, lowness can seem like a heavy burden or a place where hope is diminished and doubt begins to creep in. But it is essential to remember that lowness is not the end of our journey. Rather, it is often a stepping stone toward renewal and empowerment. In the midst of our weakness, there is a profound truth rooted in faith: Yahweh, our Creator, desires us to be strong. The Scriptures repeatedly emphasize the importance of strength, not merely physical, but spiritual and moral strength that comes from trusting in Him. Yahweh's desire is for us to rise above our lowness, to find resilience not in ourselves alone, but in His power and mercy. He calls us to be strong in faith, to stand firm in the face of adversity, and to lean on His unfailing support. Yahweh's longing for our strength is rooted in His love and His desire for us to live life abundantly. When we feel weak, He offers us His strength to carry us through difficult times. See Case Law **§ 2 Corinthians 12:9** that Yahweh's mercy is sufficient, for His power is made perfect in weakness. This means that our lowness is not a sign of failure but an opportunity to experience His divine power working within us. It is in our moments of vulnerability that Yahweh's strength is most evident, shining through to lift us up when we cannot lift ourselves. Moreover, Yahweh's call for us to be strong is also a call to faith and perseverance. Being strong in Him requires surrendering our own notions of control and trusting in His plan. It involves acknowledging our weaknesses and asking for His help. It is through reliance on His strength that we find true resilience, hope, and purpose. No matter how low we may feel, we are never beyond His reach, and His desire is for us to rise, renewed and strengthened by His love.

In recognizing lowness as a part of life, we also acknowledge our need for divine intervention. We are encouraged to seek His guidance, to pray earnestly, and to open our hearts to His restorative power. Through this reliance, our weakness transforms into a testimony of His greatness. Our lowness can become a catalyst for spiritual growth, humility, and a deeper understanding of His mercy. While lowness or the state of being weak is a natural and often unavoidable aspect of our human condition, it is not something Yahweh wants us to remain in. His desire is for us to be strong—strong in faith, strong in hope, and strong in His love. He offers us His strength to carry us through our moments of weakness and to help us emerge on the other side more resilient and closer to Him. Embracing our lowness with sincerity and trust in Yahweh's promise transforms it into a platform for His glory to be revealed in our lives. Let us remember that in our weakness, His strength is made perfect, and through Him, we can rise above any lowness that seeks to hold us down. In a world rife with temptation and moral ambiguity, it is all too easy to succumb to the darker, more base aspects of human nature. These actions which are marked by their lack of honor, spirit, and vivacity, are often tempting shortcuts that seem to offer immediate gratification but ultimately lead us away from the righteousness that Yahweh desires for His children. To be truly honorable is to live with integrity, to uphold virtues that transcend fleeting pleasures, and to recognize the divine within ourselves and others.

Yahweh, in His infinite wisdom and love, calls us to a higher standard. He desires us to act with dignity, to embody principles of honesty, compassion, and humility. It is not enough to avoid overtly evil deeds. We must actively pursue goodness and reject behaviors that are morally reprehensible and those that are selfish, deceitful, or undermining the dignity of others. When we choose actions that are base, which are those lacking in spirit, liveliness, and moral courage, we diminish ourselves and betray the divine image within us. The appeal of the base is seductive because it often offers quick, easy gains. Whether it be greed, envy, dishonesty, or cruelty, such behaviors drain life from the soul and strip away the vibrancy that comes from living in accordance with divine principles. These acts are devoid of true spirit. They lack the vitality that comes from living honorably and authentically. They are hollow pursuits that leave us feeling empty, disconnected from our purpose and from Yahweh's plan for us.

Yahweh's desire is for us to be honorable in every action, to elevate our lives through acts of kindness, justice, and mercy. Honor involves recognizing the worth of others, even when it's inconvenient or challenging. It requires courage to stand for what is right, especially when the world around us may tempt us toward complacency or moral compromise. To live honorably is to infuse our lives with zeal or an energetic commitment to goodness that lights our path and inspires those around us.

Furthermore, the presence of honor lifts our spirits. It brings a sense of fulfillment that no amount of base behavior can provide. When we act with integrity, we promote trust, respect, and peace within ourselves and in our relationships. These qualities are vital for a life well-lived and are in harmony with Yahweh's commandments. They reflect His divine nature and His desire for us to mirror His goodness.

In contrast, choosing to act in a base manner is to reject Yahweh's call for us to be honorable. It is to embrace a life devoid of enthusiasm and purpose. Such actions are morally reprehensible because they dishonor the divine image within each person and undermine the moral fabric of our communities. They sap the robustness from our spirits and leave us spiritually impoverished.

Ultimately, the path Yahweh sets before us is one of nobility and honor. It is a path that requires strength of character and a sincere commitment to living uprightly. While the temptations to lower ourselves to the level of the base are many, we must remember that true vigor and spirit are found in living according to divine truth. To do otherwise is to live a life lacking in the vibrancy that comes from aligning ourselves with Yahweh's will.

Let us strive each day to reject the base and embrace the honorable. Let us live with integrity and honor the divine within ourselves and others. In doing so, we find not only moral righteousness but also the liveliness and spirit that make life truly meaningful. Yahweh desires us to be honorable. Let us heed that call with sincerity and courage, knowing that such a life is the one that truly honors Him.

In a world where morality often seems to blur and the line between right and wrong becomes increasingly ambiguous, it is tempting to adopt a ruthless attitude that disregards principles and moral considerations in favor of self-interest, power, or convenience. Yet, as followers of Yahweh, we are called to a different standard. He desires us to be principled, to uphold justice, kindness, and morality even when it is difficult or inconvenient.

Ruthlessness, by its very nature, is characterized by a lack of concern for what is right or just. It is a way of operating that prioritizes outcomes over values, ignoring the moral standard that should guide our actions. When driven by ruthlessness, individuals may trample over others, manipulate situations, and make decisions solely based on personal gain or the desire to dominate. This approach may seem effective in the short term, but it ultimately leads to destruction of relationships, character, and even the soul.

Yahweh, however, calls us to a higher standard. The scriptures repeatedly emphasize the importance of being principled anchored in truth, justice, mercy, and humility. See Case Law **§ Proverbs 21:3** reminds us, "To do righteousness and justice is more acceptable to Yahweh than sacrifice." This indicates that our moral integrity is what truly matters in His eyes, more than external acts or appearances. Being principled means making choices based on what is right, even when it costs us personally. It means standing firm in our convictions, refusing to compromise our values for convenience or to avoid conflict.

The journey of being principled is often challenging. It can be tempting to resort to ruthlessness when faced with opposition or injustice. Sometimes, it may seem easier to cut corners or to retaliate rather than to respond with patience and kindness. Yet, Yahweh teaches us through His Word that true strength lies in humility and steadfastness. See Case Law **§ Micah 6:8**, we are instructed, "He has shown you, O mortal, what is good. And what does Yahweh require of you? To act justly and to love mercy and to walk humbly with your God Yahweh." These qualities stand in stark contrast to ruthlessness, which often stems from pride or a desire to dominate.

Furthermore, being principled involves trusting in Yahweh's justice rather than taking matters into our own hands. See Case Law **§ Romans 12:17** encourages believers to avoid revenge and to leave justice to Yahweh, "Recompense to no man evil for evil. Provide things honest in the sight of all men". Ruthless behavior may seem like a way to achieve our goals quickly, but it often leads to cycles of retaliation and further injustice. True strength, as modeled by Yahweh, is shown in patience, forgiveness, and unwavering commitment to what is right.

It is worth reflecting that Yahweh's heart is for righteousness and justice. His justice is perfect and merciful, and He desires His followers to mirror His character. This means rejecting ruthlessness and embracing principled conduct. When we choose to be principled, even in the face of opposition or temptation, we demonstrate trust in Yahweh's sovereignty and a commitment to His moral standards. Our lives become testimonies of His goodness and justice, shining light into a dark world that often celebrates cruelty.

While the world may applaud those who are ruthless and those who stop at nothing to achieve their ends, the believer's path is different. Yahweh's desire is for us to be principled, to uphold righteousness and justice, and to walk humbly with Him. Ferocity, guided by selfishness or a desire for power, is not the way of His kingdom. Instead, we are called to stand firm in our principles, trusting that Yahweh's justice will prevail. Let us remember that true strength lies in integrity, mercy, and faithfulness to our Creator's standards, even when it is difficult. In doing so, we honor Yahweh and become beacons of His righteousness in a world that desperately needs His light. The world can be unconscionable. It's a word that echoes deeply within our conscience, yet often, in the pursuits of personal gain or selfish ambition, individuals drift into actions that are unconscionable which are those that are not guided by what is right, nor show any genuine concern for others. To be unconscionable is to ignore the moral compass that should steer our decisions, to act in a way that is fundamentally unjust or cruel without remorse or restraint.

From the very beginning, there has been an understanding that we are created with a moral sense, a sense of right and wrong that points us toward goodness and justice. Many believe that this moral sense is rooted in divine guidance. Yahweh, the Creator, has made it clear through sacred teachings and commandments that we are called to live morally upright lives. His desire is not for us to act unreasonably, or violate the innate sense of justice within us, or disregard the dignity and worth of our fellow human beings.

Throughout history, holy principles have been given to help us distinguish right from wrong. These principles are meant to uphold justice, compassion, humility, and love. When we act in ways that are unconscionable whether through cruelty, greed, dishonesty, or neglect, we betray the very moral foundation that Yahweh desires for us to embody. Such actions often stem from selfishness, arrogance, or a complete indifference to the suffering of others. They reflect a departure from godlike guidance and a disregard for the moral duties we owe to one another.

It is important to recognize that being unethical is not merely about breaking rules or laws. It is about disregarding the moral code that underpins a just and compassionate society. The Laws of יהוה are perfect. But the moral principles taught by Yahweh transcend mere legality. They call us to a higher standard that cares about the well-being of others, about equity, and about the integrity of our own character. When we choose to ignore these moral teachings and act crooked, we not only harm others but also diminish our own humanity.

The sincere hope and divine desire are that we would cultivate morals rooted in love and righteousness. Yahweh's commandments serve as a moral compass, guiding us away from unethical actions and toward acts of kindness, justice, and humility. These teachings challenge us to look beyond ourselves, to consider the impact of our choices on those around us, and to act with conscience and compassion. Yet, it is painfully evident that humanity is often tempted to abandon these divine moral standards in pursuit of personal benefit or at the expense of others. This is when actions become corrupt and when they are committed without regard for what is right, just, or compassionate. Such conduct reveals a heart hardened by selfishness and a mind blinded by greed or pride.

In a world where cutthroat acts can sometimes seem commonplace and where injustice and cruelty can go unchecked, it is vital to remember that Yahweh desires us to be different. He calls us to be moral agents, to uphold justice and kindness even when it is difficult, even when others do not. Our morals are not just a set of rules but a reflection of our connection to divine goodness. To be ruthless is to forsake the moral guidance that Yahweh provides. It is to act without concern for what is right, often causing pain and injustice in the process. But we are encouraged to recognize the divine intention for us to live morally, to seek justice, and to show compassion. Through sincere effort and divine guidance, we can resist the temptation to act opportunistically and instead embody the moral virtues that bring true righteousness and peace to our communities and ourselves. In the quiet moments of reflection, when we ponder the purpose of our lives and the choices we make each day, one truth remains clear: Being good is not merely a matter of social convention or personal preference, but a moral requisite rooted in the very fabric of existence. Our journey through life is intertwined with the understanding that goodness is fundamental to harmony, growth, and the divine purpose bestowed upon us. To truly grasp why being good is so essential, we must consider the origins of goodness itself and the moral principles that guide us. Central to this understanding is the profound truth that Yahweh, the Creator of all that exists, is the source of good. From the beginning, Yahweh fashioned the universe with a deliberate intent to establish a world characterized by goodness, order, and beauty. The biblical account of creation underscores this: "Yahweh saw all that he had made, and it was very good". See Case Law **§ Genesis 1:31**. This declaration reveals that goodness is not an arbitrary attribute but an intrinsic quality woven into the very nature of creation. When Yahweh created humanity in His image (see Case Law **§ Genesis 1:27**), He endowed us with the capacity and moral responsibility to reflect that goodness through our actions, attitudes, and choices. Recognizing that goodness originates from Yahweh imposes upon us a moral obligation. We are called to mirror divine goodness, not only because it aligns us with our Creator but because it fosters a world where love, justice, compassion, and peace can flourish.

This divine blueprint for morality is not a set of restrictive rules but a pathway that leads us toward our highest potential as individuals and as a community. Living according to accepted rules of moral conduct such as honesty, kindness, humility, patience, and forgiveness, is a way of aligning ourselves with the divine purpose. It is an act of love and gratitude for the Creator Yahweh who has shown us what is good. Furthermore, the urgency to be good extends beyond personal virtue; it impacts the collective well-being of society. When individuals choose goodness, they contribute to the creation of a just and compassionate community. Conversely, when we neglect moral principles, chaos, suffering, and alienation take root. The acceptance of moral conduct is thus vital for maintaining social harmony and ensuring that each person's dignity is upheld. It is through our consistent commitment to goodness that we build bridges of trust and understanding, fostering environments where love and respect can thrive. Being good also reflects a deep understanding of our shared world. Every person bears the image of Yahweh, making every individual worthy of kindness and equity. Recognizing this divine image in others compels us to treat everyone with dignity and compassion. This moral stance is not optional but essential, for it echoes the divine love that Yahweh has for all creation. When we act with goodness, we affirm the divine presence within each person and uphold the sacredness of life itself. Moreover, embracing the importance of goodness is a testament to our faith and trust in Yahweh's plan. It demonstrates our commitment to living in accordance with divine will, even when faced with temptation or adversity. The path of moral conduct may sometimes be challenging, but it is through perseverance and sincere effort that we grow into the individuals Yahweh intends us to be. Our goodness becomes a reflection of our trust in divine wisdom and our desire to participate actively in the unfolding of divine purpose on earth. The prerequisite to be good is deeply rooted in the understanding that Yahweh, the Creator of all, is inherently good. Our moral conduct is a response to this divine goodness, a way of honoring our Creator, and aligning ourselves with the highest ideals of love, justice, and righteousness.

Living according to accepted rules of moral conduct is not only a duty but a sacred privilege. It is a reflection of our faith, our respect for others, and our commitment to creating a world that mirrors the divine goodness from which all life flows. Being good, therefore, is not simply advisable, but essential for our spiritual growth, societal harmony, and fulfillment of our divine purpose. In our journey through life, one of the most profound and essential pursuits is to become truly competent. Competence, in its deepest sense, goes beyond merely possessing knowledge or skills. It embodies a sincere dedication to excellence, integrity, and moral uprightness. When we consider our purpose in life, especially in relation to our spiritual responsibilities, the concept of being competent takes on even greater significance. We are not only active participants in the world around us; we are called to be qualified before Yahweh, our Creator and Judge. To understand what it means to be competent before Yahweh, we must first recognize that our human abilities, like our talents, intelligence, and skills, are gifts from Him. These gifts are meant to be cultivated diligently, so that we can serve with sincerity and effectiveness. Competence, therefore, is not just about personal achievement. It is about aligning ourselves with divine standards, growing in righteousness, and earning the trust of our Heavenly Father. Only then can we truly fulfill our purpose in His sight. The requirement to qualify before Yahweh is a call to sincerity and humility. It challenges us to evaluate our hearts, motives, and actions continuously. To be competent in His eyes means to develop a character that mirrors His virtues such as faithfulness, humility, love, patience, and integrity. It involves diligent study of His Word, earnest prayer, and a willingness to be molded by the Holy Spirit. Genuine competence is rooted in a heart that seeks to please Yahweh above all else, recognizing that our worth is not determined by worldly standards but by our faithfulness to His divine will. Moreover, this qualification process is ongoing. It is not a one-time achievement but a lifelong journey of growth and refinement. As we face life's trials and temptations, our competence is tested and strengthened. We learn through our successes and failures, always striving to become more aligned with Yahweh's righteousness. In doing so, we demonstrate true sincerity or an authentic desire to serve Yahweh with our whole being, not out of obligation, but out of love and devotion.

Being competent before Yahweh also entails responsibility. We are entrusted with talents and resources, and we are accountable for how we handle them. This accountability calls for us to develop our capabilities, to act wisely, and to uphold justice and mercy. Our competence is revealed in our consistency, our perseverance, and our willingness to improve in humility. It is about diligently working to become vessels of honor, fit for divine use. In the end, the path to competence before Yahweh is paved with sincerity. It is a heartfelt pursuit rooted in the understanding that our efforts are ultimately for His glory. The more we dedicate ourselves to this pursuit (studying His Word, living out His commandments, and cultivating a character that reflects His love), the more qualified we become in His sight. This qualification is not simply about meeting a standard. It is about embracing a way of life that honours Yahweh in all we do.

Therefore, let us approach this journey with humility and earnestness. Let us remember that our competence is not just for our benefit but for Yahweh's Kingdom. As we seek to qualify before Yahweh, may we do so with sincerity, recognizing that true competence is a reflection of our commitment to live according to His divine purpose. In this pursuit, we find not only our greatest fulfillment, but also the assurance that we are aligning ourselves with the divine will and are becoming truly fitted for the purpose Yahweh has designed for us. The nature of Yahweh as a Creator is profoundly rooted in logic and reason. When contemplating the origins of the universe, it becomes evident that invoking a divine Creator who is inherently logical offers a coherent and satisfying explanation for the existence and order of everything around us. Yahweh, as understood through many theological and philosophical perspectives, is not a capricious or arbitrary being but a rational, purposeful Creator whose existence and actions align with principles of logic and reason. Firstly, the very act of creation presupposes a rational plan. If we consider the universe as a product of intelligent design, then the underlying order and consistency we observe such as the laws of physics, the fine-tuning of constants, and the intricate complexity of biological systems, are indicative of a creator who possesses deliberate intention.

It is unreasonable to assume that such precise harmony and structure could arise from chaos or uncertainty alone. Instead, the logical inference points toward an intelligent mind capable of establishing and maintaining these laws. Furthermore, Yahweh's nature as a logical Creator is consistent with the idea of a rational mind behind existence. The notion that the universe operates according to comprehensible laws implies that its Creator must also be rational. It would be inconsistent for an irrational or non-thinking entity to create a universe governed by logic and order. The coherence of natural laws and the comprehensibility of the universe reflect the rationality of the Creator, implying that Yahweh embodies perfect wisdom and understanding.

Additionally, the moral and ethical dimensions of human existence further support the idea of a logical Creator. The innate sense of justice, morality, and purpose within human beings hints at a divine moral lawgiver who instilled these qualities. Such moral principles are not random but are grounded in reason and rationality. A logical Creator would establish moral standards that are consistent, universal, and intelligible, guiding human behavior toward harmony and purpose.

Moreover, the existence of human consciousness and the capacity for rational thought itself are compelling indicators of a logical Creator. Human beings possess the ability to reason, analyze, and seek understanding which are traits that suggest they were designed with intellect and consciousness in mind. The very faculties of logic and reason that humans wield are reflective of the Creator's own rational nature.

Sincerity in understanding Yahweh as a logical Creator also involves recognizing that faith and reason are not mutually exclusive but complementary. Many spiritual traditions affirm that divine truths can be apprehended through reason, and that understanding the universe's rational structure is a step toward appreciating the divine intelligence behind it. Embracing this point of view promotes a humble acknowledgment that our reasoning, though finite, is a reflection of the infinite wisdom of Yahweh.

Viewing Yahweh as a logical Creator aligns with the observable order of the universe, the rational laws governing nature, and the moral fabric of human life. It offers a logical framework that bridges faith and reason, encouraging sincere pursuit of understanding the divine. Recognizing the logical nature of Yahweh affirms that belief in a rational Creator is not only a matter of faith but also a conclusion drawn from sound reasoning and the evidence of the universe itself. Loyalty is a profound and unchangable commitment that goes beyond mere words or brief feelings. It is the steady anchor of our relationships, beliefs, and convictions, guiding us through life's challenges and uncertainties. To be loyal means to stand firm in one's allegiance, to remain steadfast regardless of the circumstances, and to prioritize the well-being and honor of whom or what we are committed to. Genuine loyalty is a testament to character; It reflects integrity, trustworthiness, and a deep sense of responsibility. At the heart of true loyalty lies an unwavering trust and devotion. When we are loyal, we choose to support and defend, not because it is convenient or easy, but because we believe in the value and importance of the relationship or cause. Loyalty requires sacrifice, patience, and resilience. It demands that we remain committed even when faced with difficulties, temptations, or doubts. True loyalty is not fake or conditional. It is a deep-seated conviction that persists through ups and downs. Among the most profound examples of loyalty in history and faith is the loyalty of Yahweh. In many spiritual customs, Yahweh is regarded as the ultimate symbol of unwavering devotion and steadfast love. Throughout sacred texts, Yahweh's loyalty is depicted as infinite and unchanging. Despite humanity's shortcomings, failures, and rebellions, Yahweh remains faithful. This divine loyalty offers a model for us all as a reminder that true fidelity is rooted in unconditional love and commitment. Yahweh's loyalty is evident in His promises and His consistent presence. When Yahweh makes a covenant, He keeps it. His loyalty endures through generations, through times of prosperity and hardship alike. His faithfulness is not dependent on human actions. It is an unwavering stance rooted in divine love and integrity. This steadfastness inspires believers to mirror such loyalty in their own lives and to be loyal to their faith, their principles, and their loved ones with the same unwavering devotion.

In a world where loyalties can often be fickle or fake, the loyalty of Yahweh stands as a beacon of stability and hope. It reminds us that true allegiance is a choice or a conscious decision to remain committed, to uphold what is right, and to love unconditionally. To be loyal in the truest sense, is to mirror that divine example, stand firm in our commitments, support others faithfully, and to uphold our values even when faced with adversity. Loyalty is a powerful virtue that defines character and integrity. It calls us to remain firm and steadfast in our allegiances, to honor our commitments with sincerity and resilience. Yahweh exemplifies the highest form of loyalty; He is unwavering, eternal, and divine. As followers and individuals striving to live meaningful lives, we are encouraged to mirror this divine loyalty, to be faithful not only in words but in deeds, and to hold fast to what we believe is true and right. True loyalty is a gift we give to others and to the divine, a testament to the strength of our convictions and the depth of our love. When we consider the concept of being skilled, we are exploring more than mere competence or proficiency. True skill embodies a deep understanding, a mastery that is often built through years of dedicated effort, perseverance, and a genuine passion for one's craft. It reflects an exceptional knowledge and experience that allows an individual to navigate complex situations with confidence, elegance, and insight. In many ways, being skilled is a testament to a commitment to excellence, and a constant pursuit of growth that often aligns with moral and spiritual values.

At the heart of this understanding is the recognition that true skill is not solely about technical ability or external achievements. It often encompasses a moral dimension, especially when viewed through a spiritual lens. For instance, Yahweh, the divine presence in many faith values, is often understood as embodying goodness, righteousness, and justice. His nature is fundamentally good, standing for what is right and just. This divine goodness serves as a model for those who seek to develop their skills not just for personal gain but in service of good. When we think of Yahweh as good and as representative of good, we recognize that true skill is ultimately rooted in integrity, humility, and a sincere desire to contribute positively to the world.

An individual who possesses genuine skill, guided by moral principles, acts with kindness, patience, and a sense of responsibility toward others. Such a person understands that mastery is a gift that carries with it the obligation to uplift, to serve, and to act in accordance with what is righteous. Furthermore, skilled individuals often demonstrate a humility grounded in the awareness that their abilities are not solely their own but are also a reflection of divine mercy and guidance. They acknowledge that their talents and knowledge are part of a larger divine plan, and they seek to use their skills to promote goodness, justice, and compassion. This perspective produces a sincere humility that keeps their pursuits aligned with higher moral standards.

In the context of faith and spirituality, being truly skilled involves a deep spiritual discipline and cultivating not only technical expertise but also moral virtues. It requires patience to refine one's craft, humility to learn from others, and a heartfelt commitment to serving others in love and truth. These qualities mirror the divine attributes exemplified by Yahweh (goodness, mercy, righteousness), ensuring that their skills do not become tools for selfishness or arrogance, but are instead channels for divine goodness. Moreover, this divine model reminds us that the highest form of skill is one that uplifts others and promotes the greater good. It is about using one's expertise to heal, teach, guide, and serve always with a sincere heart and a desire to reflect divine goodness. Such an outlook elevates the concept of skill from mere competence to a moral and spiritual calling, which is a way to embody the virtues that Yahweh exemplifies. Being skilled is not just about possessing exceptional knowledge or experience. It is about aligning one's abilities with moral virtues, humility, and a sincere desire to serve the greater good. Yahweh's goodness and his standing for what is right serve as a profound model for those who seek to develop and use their skills in a way that truly benefits others. When skill is rooted in goodness and guided by divine principles, it transforms from mere competence into a powerful force for positive change which is an expression of love, righteousness, and divine purpose.

This world is filled with choices, but one path stands out as the true course of purpose and fulfillment: choosing good. From the very beginning, Yahweh, the Creator of all, designed us with a divine intention to embody goodness. Our very nature reflects His image, calling us to live with integrity, kindness, and compassion.

Choosing good is not simply a moral obligation. It is an affirmation of our inherent divine purpose. When we opt for what is right, we align ourselves with Yahweh's original design, promoting harmony within ourselves and with those around us. Every act of goodness reinforces the truth that we are meant to uplift, serve, and contribute positively to the world.

Moreover, welcoming goodness builds trust and credibility. It empowers us to lead by example, inspiring others to follow the righteous path. Confidence in choosing good, stems from knowing we are fulfilling the higher calling given to us by the Creator Yahweh. It's a confident stand rooted in faith that doing right is ultimately the most rewarding and impactful choice.

In essence, choosing good is a proclamation of our divine identity and purpose. It affirms that we are made to be good, to bring light into darkness, and to integrate the love Yahweh has for all creation. Make the conscious decision today to choose to be good, and walk confidently on the path that leads to true fulfillment and eternal purpose.

Chapter 7

In our journey through life, we often seek recognition, approval, or admiration from others. Yet, at the core of genuine fulfillment is the understanding that the highest form of praise comes from Yahweh, our Creator. He desires for us to exude qualities and characteristics that are truly meritorious or worthy of high regard and great approval, not for the sake of human accolades but because such traits reflect His divine nature within us.

Yahweh, in His infinite wisdom and love, calls us to embody virtues that elevate our character and bring glory to His name. These qualities such as kindness, humility, integrity, patience, and compassion, are not merely societal ideals but are rooted in His divine commandments and teachings. When we strive to develop and demonstrate these traits, we align ourselves more closely with His will and become living testimonies of His goodness.

To be praiseworthy, therefore, requires a sincere effort to cultivate a heart that is humble and a spirit that is earnest in doing what is right. It calls us to look beyond superficial appearances and to seek a genuine inner transformation that manifests through our words, actions, and attitudes. Yahweh wants us to demonstrate love not only outwardly but also inwardly, allowing His divine love to flow through us and touch those around us.

Living in a way that is deserving of high regard also involves accountability and a constant reevaluation of our motives. Are our actions driven by a desire to serve and honor Yahweh, or are they motivated by self-interest or pride? The path to being praiseworthy is not paved with perfection but with humility and a sincere willingness to grow, learn, and improve each day.

Moreover, the pursuit of admirable characteristics is a reflection of our gratitude for the mercy and kindness that Yahweh has extended to us. Recognizing His patience and unconditional love inspires us to mirror those qualities in our interactions with others. When we act with integrity and sincerity, we position ourselves as worthy vessels for His blessings and as examples of His transformative power. It is important to remember that Yahweh's assessment of our worthiness is rooted in sincerity rather than superficial appearances. He looks into our hearts and understands our intentions better than anyone. Therefore, cultivating a praiseworthy character requires honesty with ourselves and a genuine desire to please Him above all else. Being deserving of high regard or great approval is not about seeking recognition from others but about living in a way that reflects the divine virtues Yahweh desires for us. It involves earnest effort, humility, and a heart committed to righteousness. When we align our lives with His will and allow His Spirit to guide us, our lives become a testament to His goodness, and worthy of praise, admiration, and honor in His sight. Let us strive daily to embody these praiseworthy qualities, knowing that in doing so, we bring joy to our Creator and fulfill the purpose for which we were made. When we consider the concept of being worthy, we are delving into a profound truth that extends beyond surface appearances or brief accomplishments. To be worthy is to possess a depth of character, integrity, and genuine virtue that stands firm even amid life's uncertainties. It is about more than just meeting expectations; it is about embodying qualities that earn respect, admiration, and appreciation over time. True worthiness is rooted in sincerity, consistency, and a commitment to principles that transcend personal gain. It is built through deliberate effort, perseverance, and a sincere passion for one's purpose, much like the development of true skill. In the realm of spiritual truth and faith, this concept of worthiness takes on an even more significant dimension. When we speak of Yahweh Almighty as worthy, we acknowledge a divine excellence that surpasses human understanding. Yahweh is worthy of praise and honor not because of any superficial or temporary attribute, but because of His eternal nature, His unwavering goodness, and His infinite mercy. His worthiness is essential, deep-rooted in His perfection, sovereignty, and love.

To recognize Yahweh as worthy is to admit that His majesty and power are deserving of our deepest respect and devotion. It is to understand that His attributes like mercy, justice, faithfulness, and sovereignty, are qualities that command admiration and heartfelt gratitude from every living soul. Worshiping Yahweh becomes not merely a duty but a sincere act born out of recognizing His supreme worthiness. When we lift our voices in praise or bow our knees in humility, we are expressing the acknowledgment that no one and nothing else compares to Yahweh's divine majesty.

Furthermore, the sincerity of our praise is what truly honors Yahweh's worthiness. Genuine worship arises from a heart that truly understands and appreciates who Yahweh is. It involves more than outer rituals. It is about aligning our lives with the truth that Yahweh is deserving of all honor, all glory, and all devotion. This recognition should inspire us to live with integrity, humility, and love which are qualities that reflect Yahweh's character and demonstrate that we truly value who He is.

In our journey toward understanding worthiness, we also realize that it is something we develop through our actions, attitudes, and choices. Like true skill, being worthy involves effort, perseverance, and an earnest desire to grow in righteousness. It requires humility to acknowledge our dependence on divine grace and a sincere passion to honor Yahweh in all we do. As we strive to be worthy in our daily lives, we mirror the divine worthiness that is demonstrated through His love and mercy.

Ultimately, when we consider Yahweh as worthy of praise and honor, we are invited into a heartfelt acknowledgment that elevates our spirits and deepens our relationship with the divine. It is a call to live with sincerity, recognizing that true worthiness is rooted in the divine nature of Yahweh Himself. In doing so, we find that our lives are transformed and become testimonies of genuine devotion, humility, and honor for the One who is truly worthy of all praise.

In our journey through life, there is an innate desire within each of us to be recognized and accepted for who we truly are. This desire often manifests as a longing to establish ourselves or our character, our purpose, our relationship with the Divine. Among all the relationships we seek to build, none is as crucial and sacred as our connection with Yahweh, the Creator of all. To truly establish ourselves before Him is to attain His full recognition and acceptance, a goal that requires sincere effort, humility, and unwavering faith.

Establishing ourselves before Yahweh is not just about outward appearances or false gestures. It is about proving our heart, our integrity, and our devotion. It involves a deliberate and persistent effort to align our lives with Yahweh's commandments and His divine will. We must recognize that Yahweh is a righteous and just Yahweh, who observes the intents of our hearts and the sincerity of our actions. Therefore, our goal should be to present ourselves before Him in truth and humility, demonstrating that our desire is to walk in His ways wholeheartedly.

The first step in establishing ourselves before Yahweh is to understand that recognition from Him is a gift embedded in genuine faith and obedience. We cannot simply perform customs or say the right words expecting His acceptance. True acknowledgment from Yahweh requires more. It demands an honest evaluation of our lives, acknowledging our shortcomings and actively seeking Yahweh's forgiveness and guidance. We must prove ourselves through consistent actions that reflect our love and respect for Him. This means living with integrity, showing kindness, practicing humility, and striving to embody His teachings in our daily lives.

Proving ourselves to Yahweh is also a matter of perseverance. It is easy to be faithful during times of blessing and comfort, but true establishment is tested during trials and hardships. When faced with challenges, we are called to remain steadfast, trusting that Yahweh's plan is perfect and that our unwavering devotion will earn His recognition. Every act of faithfulness, no matter how small, contributes to building a solid foundation of trust and acceptance in Yahweh's eyes.

Furthermore, establishing ourselves before Yahweh involves forming a genuine relationship. Prayer, study of Yahweh's Word, and meditative reflection are powerful ways to deepen our connection. Through these disciplines, we gain insight into His character and commands, enabling us to better align ourselves with Yahweh's will. As we grow in knowledge and love for Yahweh, our sincerity becomes more evident, and our efforts to establish ourselves before Yahweh become more heartfelt and meaningful. And actually mean something.

We must also remember that Yahweh desires a relationship built on sincerity rather than facade. He is merciful and compassionate, willing to accept our efforts when they are driven by genuine love and humility. Our goal is to attain perfection on our own but to continually seek Yahweh's mercy and to present ourselves before Him as imperfect beings striving to improve. It is through Yahweh's mercy that we are able to be established and fully recognized.

Establishing ourselves before Yahweh is a sacred and ongoing process that requires sincerity, effort, and unwavering faith. It involves proving our devotion through actions and attitudes that reflect our love for Him. We must humble ourselves, acknowledge our shortcomings, and seek Yahweh's forgiveness and guidance. As we persevere in faith and obedience, we move closer to the full recognition and acceptance that Yahweh offers to those who sincerely seek to walk in His truth. Ultimately, our goal is to be seen by Yahweh as faithful children, fully established and accepted in His sight, reflecting His glory and love in all that we do. Throughout human history, countless cultures and individuals have sought to understand the origins of morality, the foundation of right and wrong, and the existence of a higher power that governs and sustains moral order. One compelling line of evidence that points to the existence of Yahweh, the divine Creator, is the observable reality of moral behavior among spiritual beings. In examining the nature of morality, we find that it is not merely a social construct or a product of evolutionary processes but rather a reflection of a divine moral law fixed in the character of Yahweh Himself.

Moral behavior like acts of kindness, justice, compassion, honesty, and self-control, are more than just community ideals. They serve as evidence of a divine moral lawgiver. The very fact that humans possess an innate sense of right and wrong, that they are capable of choosing good over evil, suggests an outer standard or an ultimate source of moral goodness. Without such a standard, morality would be reduced to subjective preferences or societal conventions that vary across cultures and eras. However, the universality and consistency of fundamental moral principles point to a divine origin. In the Hebrew custom, it is taught that Yahweh is the ultimate standard of morality. The moral behavior exhibited by individuals and communities aligns with His character (truthfulness, justice, mercy, and love), serving as evidence of Yahweh's existence. When people act morally, they reflect qualities that are consistent with the divine nature. For instance, acts of sacrificial love, genuine kindness, and unwavering justice are not random or aimless. They mirror the moral attributes of Yahweh Himself. Such behaviors, observed across diverse societies and historical periods, serve as a testament to the presence of a moral lawgiver who instills these qualities within humanity. Furthermore, the existence of moral conscience or an inner awareness of right and wrong, is another powerful piece of evidence supporting Yahweh's existence. Many people, regardless of their literacy background, experience a sense of guilt or shame when they do wrong, and a feeling of peace or fulfillment when they do good. This conscience is not solely a product of lifestyle conditioning but appears to be an innate part of human nature, pointing to a divine imprint. The moral compass within humans indicates that morality is not accidental but intentionally embedded by a moral Creator Yahweh, who desires humans to live according to His standards. The consistency of moral behavior across different cultures and times also provides compelling evidence. While specific customs and beliefs may vary, there is a remarkable convergence on core moral values such as justice, mercy, and integrity. This combination suggests an underlying universal moral law, which many theologians and philosophers attribute to Yahweh's moral character. The fact that humans, created in the image of Yahweh, naturally recognize and strive toward these moral truths further supports the idea that moral behavior is entrenched in a divine source.

Moreover, history demonstrates that moral progress like advancements in justice, human rights, and ethical standards, are driven by a recognition of moral principles that transcend individual or societal interests. These moral advancements often stem from the influence of spiritual teachings, including those about Yahweh, which emphasize the inherent dignity of every person and the importance of justice and compassion. Such moral progress, inspired by divine moral truths, acts as evidence of a divine moral law that guides human development toward higher ethical standards. The existence and consistent presence of moral behavior among humans serve as a profound and compelling form of evidence for the existence of Yahweh. The moral conscience implanted within us, the universality of moral principles, and the moral progress throughout history all point toward a divine moral lawgiver. Recognizing morality as evidence of Yahweh's existence requires an open heart and mind to see beyond mere physical and material explanations, embracing the idea that moral behavior reflects the character and existence of the divine. This understanding provides not only a foundation for believing in Yahweh but also inspires humans to live in accordance with the moral truths that point us back to our Creator Yahweh. There comes a time when we must pause and reflect on our purpose and the impact we have on those around us. To elevate oneself is not merely a matter of personal growth or achievement; it is about standing tall in integrity, humility, and faith so that others may see the example we set and be inspired to serve Yahweh wholcheartedly. Truly, our lives are a mirror reflecting His love, His mercy, and His commandments. When we elevate ourselves in righteousness, we become illumines of light guiding others toward a closer relationship with the Divine. To serve Yahweh with sincerity requires more than words; it demands action rooted in genuine belief. We are called to be living testimonies of Yahweh's goodness, showing that faith is not just something to believe in silently, but something to embody daily. As Scripture reminds us, "Let your light so shine before men, that they may see your good works, and glorify your Father Yahweh which is in heaven" see Case Law **§ Matthew 5:16**. Our conduct, our choices, and our attitude should elevate us from worldly temptations and fake pursuits, anchoring us firmly in Yahweh's truth.

Setting an example is an esoteric responsibility. When we elevate ourselves in humility and obedience, we serve as catalysts for others to do the same. Our unwavering commitment to Yahweh's commandments demonstrates that true strength is found in surrendering to His will, not in arrogance or self-reliance. It is through our actions such as showing kindness, patience, humility, and unwavering faith, that we reveal the character of Yahweh to those who may have drifted away or are seeking a deeper connection. Furthermore, elevating oneself involves constant self-awareness and self-improvement. It means acknowledging our shortcomings and seeking divine guidance to become better servants of Yahweh. This continuous effort not only enriches our spiritual lives but also sets a powerful example for our nation. When others see us striving to live according to Yahweh's Word, they are more likely to be encouraged to do the same. Our lives become testimonies of Yahweh's transformative power, demonstrating that change is possible, and serving Yahweh is the highest calling we can pursue. It's important to remember that elevating ourselves is not about personal glorification. Instead, it is about magnifying Yahweh through our conduct and words. Our elevated posture both spiritually and morally, serves as a testament that faith is active, alive, and impactful. By living upright, with integrity and devotion, we serve as living proof that Yahweh's commandments are beneficial and life-giving. In the end, our goal is to inspire others to serve Yahweh with sincerity and devotion. We do this by being consistent in our walk, by demonstrating love and compassion, and by holding ourselves accountable to higher standards. When we choose to elevate ourselves in mind, body, and spirit, we create a ripple effect that encourages others to rise above their circumstances and pursue a life aligned with Yahweh's purpose. So, let us commit anew to elevating ourselves each day. Let us be the examples that others look up to, not in arrogance, but in humility and love. Through our upright stance, rooted in faith and righteousness, we can serve as guiding lights, helping others find their way to Yahweh. In doing so, we fulfill our divine calling and contribute to a world where Yahweh's glory is reflected in every life touched by our example.

Healing is a deep journey that leads us from brokenness to wholeness and from pain to peace. It is a process of restoration, not merely of the body, but of the soul and spirit as well. In the midst of life's trials and tribulations, we often seek quick fixes or temporary relief. Yet, true healing both lasting and genuine, begins with recognizing the fundamental truth that the word of Yahweh is what allows us to heal. The scriptures powerfully affirm that Yahweh, our Creator, is the Great Healer. Yahweh's word is alive and active, sharper than any two-edged sword. See Case Law **§ Hebrews 4:12**. It possesses the divine power to mend broken hearts, restore weary spirits, and renew our strength. When we immerse ourselves in Yahweh's Word, we open the door for His healing mercy to flow into every area of our lives. Yahweh promises are steadfast, and His love is unfailing. Through His Word, we find the assurance that we are not alone in our struggles. Healing begins with faith, believing that Yahweh's word is true, and that His power is sufficient to restore us. As we read and meditate on scripture, our faith is nurtured and strengthened. For example, when we cling to the promise found in see Case Law **§ Isaiah 53:5**, "But he *was* wounded for our transgressions, *he was* bruised for our iniquities: the chastisement of our peace *was* upon him; and with his stripes we are healed," we acknowledge that the suffering on the cross was not only for our salvation but also for our physical and emotional healing. The word of Yahweh gives us hope in the darkest moments, reminding us that our wounds can be healed through His divine touch. Furthermore, healing is a holistic process. It involves the renewal of mind, body, and spirit. The word of Yahweh offers wisdom on how to live in harmony with His design, guiding us toward healthy choices, forgiving those who have wronged us, and releasing bitterness and resentment that hinder our healing. See Case Law **§ Psalm 103:2-3** encourages us: "Bless the LORD Yahweh, O my soul, and forget not all his benefits: 3. Who forgiveth all thine iniquities; who healeth all thy diseases." Recognizing that Yahweh is the ultimate source of healing, we turn our hearts fully toward Him, surrendering our burdens and trusting in Yahweh's timing and plan. Restoring health also requires patience and perseverance. Healing may not happen overnight, but through consistent engagement with Yahweh's Word, we position ourselves to receive His divine healing. Prayer, worship, and scripture study become essential tools in this process. As we speak Yahweh promises over ourselves and declare His truths, our faith grows stronger, and our healing accelerates.

It is important to remember that healing is not always about the elimination of every pain or difficulty immediately. Sometimes, the healing process involves learning to endure, to forgive, and to trust that Yahweh is working everything together for our good, see Case Law **§ Romans 8:28**. Yahweh's Word sustains us through these challenges, offering comfort and assurance that His plans are perfect, and His timing is always right. Ultimately, restoration to health is about transformation from the inside out. Yahweh's Word has the power to renew our minds, revive our bodies, and restore our spirits. When we align ourselves with His truth, allow His word to dwell richly in our hearts, and trust in His divine capacity to heal, we position ourselves to experience complete restoration.

Let us then commit ourselves anew to the study and meditation of Yahweh's Word. Let us believe in its power to heal and to restore. And let us walk confidently in the assurance that Yahweh, through His Word, is actively restoring us to a healthy, vibrant, and joyful life that reflects His glory and His love. In His perfect timing, as we seek Yahweh with all our hearts, we will find healing that is whole, lasting, and complete. In a world filled with countless voices competing for attention, it is both a privilege and an outright responsibility for us to promote Yahweh who is the Creator of heaven and earth, the source of all life, love, and hope. As followers of faith, we are entrusted with a divine duty not only to believe in Yahweh but to actively share His goodness, His mercy, and His truth with others. This is not just a call. It is a sacred obligation rooted in love, humility, and a deep desire to bring light into the darkness that often surrounds us.

Promoting Yahweh is more than spreading sacred teachings. It is about embodying and reflecting His attributes like compassion, kindness, patience, and justice, in our daily lives. Through our words, actions, and attitudes, we have the opportunity to be living testimonies of Yahweh's greatness. Every act of kindness, every moment of patience, and every effort to serve others is, in essence, a form of promotion and a way of shining Yahweh's light into the lives of those who may have yet to experience His mercy.

It is essential to recognize that promoting Yahweh is our personal responsibility. It is a calling that surpasses mere obligation. It is a heartfelt response to the love we have received. When we share Yahweh's message, we are participating in a divine mission to bring hope to the hopeless, comfort to the brokenhearted, and salvation to those who seek understanding. Our words can inspire someone to seek His presence, and our actions can demonstrate His love in tangible ways.

Furthermore, promoting Yahweh requires sincerity. It is not about mere words or fake gestures but about genuine reflection of His character in our lives. When we speak about Yahweh, let our words be full of truth and humility. When we act in Yahweh's name, let our actions be motivated by authentic love and a sincere desire to serve. This sincerity adds power and credibility to our testimony, enabling others to see the transformative power of Yahweh through us.

In our efforts to promote Yahweh, we must remember that it is ultimately the work of the Holy Spirit to touch hearts and open minds. Our role is to be faithful messengers, faithful in sharing Yahweh's Word, sincere in our living examples, and persistent in our love. It is through our collective efforts, rooted in genuine devotion, that His kingdom can be further established on earth.

Let us embrace this responsibility with humility and purpose. Let us speak of Yahweh with respect and sincerity, knowing that our words and deeds can ripple outward to touch lives in ways we may never fully realize. By promoting Yahweh, we participate in a divine plan to bring salvation, hope, and everlasting love to a world desperately in need of His mercy.

In the end, it is our duty and our greatest privilege to promote Yahweh. To do so is to live out His laws, statues, judgments and commandments, to honor His Name Yahweh, and to share His eternal love with everyone around us. May our lives be a testament to Yahweh's goodness, and may our efforts to promote Yahweh inspire others to seek and find the boundless mercy and grace of our Lord Yahweh.

Each of us longs for growth, progress, and a higher place of influence and purpose. We seek to rise above challenges, limitations, and circumstances that attempt to hold us back. Yet, true elevation that brings lasting fulfillment and divine purpose, comes from a higher power. It is not merely about personal effort or ambition, but about trusting in Yahweh, the One who has the power to lift us up from the depths and set us on a higher ground. When you feel stuck or overwhelmed, remember this absolute truth: Yahweh will cause you to be elevated. His plan for your life is designed to bring you into a place of increased blessing, influence, and purpose. Yahweh's timing is perfect, and His methods are rooted in love and wisdom. It is in trusting Yahweh's sovereignty that we find the assurance that no matter how difficult the climb may seem, Yahweh is the One who will enable you to ascend to heights you never thought possible. Throughout Scripture, we see evidence of Yahweh's power to elevate His people. From Joseph being raised from the prison to becoming a ruler in Egypt, to David rising from a humble shepherd boy to the king of Israel, divine elevation is a recurring theme. These stories remind us that Yahweh's favor is not limited by our current circumstances or past mistakes. Instead, His elevation is based on His mercy, purpose, and divine timing. When Yahweh causes you to be elevated, it is always for a purpose greater than yourself, so that you may fulfill your destiny and bring glory to Yahweh's name. In your life today, you may face obstacles that seem insurmountable. You might feel overlooked or undervalued, questioning whether your efforts will ever be recognized or rewarded. It's important to hold onto the truth that Yahweh sees you, cares for you, and has a plan to lift you up. Yahweh's elevation is not unreasonable. It is a divine act rooted in His love and His desire to see His children flourish. To experience such elevation, acquires a sincere faith in Yahweh's promises. Pray earnestly, trusting that Yahweh will direct your steps and open doors of opportunity. Walk in integrity, humility, and perseverance, knowing that your character is being refined for the elevation that is to come. Remember that elevation is not just about reaching a higher position but about growing in maturity, wisdom, and purpose, as well as becoming a vessel through which Yahweh's goodness is demonstrated. Beloved, do not be discouraged when the process seems slow or when setbacks occur. Trust that Yahweh is working behind the scenes for your good.

Yahweh's Word assures us that when we seek His kingdom and righteousness, all other things will be added unto us. As you remain faithful and obedient to Yahweh, His divine favor will cause you to be elevated at the right time and in His perfect way. So, lift your eyes and your heart with hope. Believe that Yahweh will cause you to be elevated, not in arrogance or pride, but in humility and gratitude, acknowledging that your true elevation comes from Yahweh alone. Yahweh is the One who raises the humble, exalts the meek, and sets the lowly in high places. Trust in Yahweh's divine power, and walk forward with confidence, knowing that your elevation is on its way because Yahweh Himself has declared it so. Hold fast to this truth: Yahweh will cause you to be elevated. His love, power, and divine plan are working in your favor. As you submit your life to Him and remain steadfast in faith, you will ascend to the heights He has prepared for you. Be encouraged, for your elevation is not just a possibility. It is a promise rooted in the character and faithfulness of Yahweh. Walk in hope and expectation, for your time to rise is coming. There are times in life when we feel stuck, look around, and wonder if we will ever rise above our current circumstances. We may dream of climbing higher, reaching new heights, or experiencing a greater purpose. Yet, amidst our efforts and aspirations, it is vital to remember this sound truth: Only Yahweh, the Creator of heaven and earth, can truly raise us from our lowest places to the highest peaks. In our human strength, we often try to elevate ourselves through our achievements, talents, or relentless determination. We chase after success, recognition, and comfort, hoping that these will lift us up. But no matter how hard we try, true elevation that is lasting and meaningful, is beyond our power alone. Temporary gains may come, but lasting elevation, true rising, is a divine work. Only Yahweh has the authority and power to lift us from the depths of despair or the valleys of discouragement to the heights of purpose, hope, and joy. When we face moments of humility or hardship, it is tempting to feel abandoned or forgotten. Yet, even in those dark valleys, Yahweh is present. Yahweh sees our struggles and hears our cries. It is in these moments that Yahweh invites us to trust Him to raise us up. "The LORD Yahweh lifteth up the meek: He casteth the wicked down to the ground," see Case Law **§ Psalm 147:6** assures us. This lifting is not simply about physical elevation but about spiritual renewal, emotional healing, and restoration of rank. Yahweh's raising is a divine act rooted in His love, mercy, and sovereignty.

Only Yahweh can raise us to a higher place because He is the Source of all life and power. Yahweh knows our true potential, the plans He has for us, and the purpose He has set before us. When we surrender our attempts to elevate ourselves and instead place our trust in Him, we align ourselves with His divine will. In doing so, we open the door for Yahweh's power to move in our lives, lifting us beyond our limitations and elevating us to the destiny He has prepared. This process of rising is not always quick or easy. Sometimes, it involves humility, patience, and unwavering faith. It may mean enduring hardships or waiting in silence, trusting that Yahweh's timing is perfect. But through it all, we can be confident that Yahweh is at work. Yahweh lifts up the humble, exalts the lowly, and sets our feet upon solid ground. When the world seeks to bring us down or keep us in a place of despair, we have the assurance that only Yahweh can truly raise us up. So, to everyone seeking a higher place whether in your spirit, your circumstances, or your calling, remember this: Your elevation is ultimately in the hands of Yahweh. Yahweh is the One who can lift you from the depths and set your feet on the heights. Trust in Yahweh's power, His love, and His divine timing. Surrender your efforts and anxieties to Yahweh, and watch as He works a miracle of elevation in your life. Let your heart be encouraged today. No matter how low you feel or how impossible it seems to rise, Yahweh's mercy is greater. Yahweh specializes in raising the fallen, restoring the broken, and elevating those who are humble before Him. With faith and obedience, you can confidently move forward, knowing that the Lord Yahweh is the only One who can truly raise you to a higher place. And when Yahweh does, you will stand in awe of His goodness and mercy, giving Him all the glory for the elevation that only He can provide. The pursuit of excellence is a noble and constant journey, rooted in the desire to serve with integrity, skill, and dedication. To be an expert in any field of endeavor is to possess a level of knowledge, experience, and mastery that transcends average understanding. It is a testament not only to one's innate abilities but also to the unwavering commitment to growth and the continuous pursuit of improvement. In essence, an expert is someone who has dedicated themselves to understanding their craft deeply, refining their skills relentlessly, and applying their knowledge with precision and wisdom. Yahweh can turn you into an expert.

However, as believers in Yahweh, we are called to a higher standard that elevates our pursuits beyond personal achievement to a reflection of divine purpose. Yahweh, the Creator of all, requires us to become exceptional in all that we do. This call to excellence is not merely about achieving recognition or worldly success. It is about honoring Yahweh through our competence, dedication, and integrity. When we strive to excel, we mirror Yahweh's own perfection and demonstrate our commitment to living out His will in every aspect of our lives. Becoming an expert is not an overnight feat. It demands sincerity of heart, humility in our learning, and perseverance amid challenges. It entails a genuine desire to understand deeply, to grow continuously, and to serve diligently. Yahweh requires us to do everything with excellence, not for our own glory but as an act of worship and obedience: "And whatsoever ye do, do *it* heartily, as to the Lord Yahweh, and not unto men", see Case Law **§ Colossians 3:23**. This scripture reminds us that our pursuit of mastery should be motivated by a sincere desire to honor Yahweh, recognizing that our skills and knowledge are gifts meant to be used for His glory. Furthermore, excellence does not mean perfectionism or arrogance. Instead, it involves a sincere commitment to doing our best, learning from failures, and remaining humble in our achievements. An expert recognizes that mastery is a continuous journey, always seeking to improve, always acknowledging that there is more to learn. In this way, our pursuit aligns with the divine expectation that we grow in wisdom, understanding, and skill which causes us to become more like Yahweh in our character and conduct. Yahweh's requirement for us to become exceptional in all we do extends beyond professional skills. It encompasses our relationships, our service to others, and our contributions to the community. When we dedicate ourselves to excellence in every area, we become vessels through which Yahweh's love, truth, and mercy are manifested. Our work becomes a testament to His goodness, and our lives reflect His divine purpose. To be an expert is to embody a sincere dedication to mastery or a dedication that aligns with Yahweh's call for us to excel in all aspects of life.

It is about more than personal achievement. It is about honoring Yahweh through our skills, our integrity, and our steady commitment to growth. By pursuing excellence with sincerity and humility, we fulfill Yahweh's divine purpose and become true reflections of His divine nature, inspiring others to seek their own paths of mastery settled in faith and devotion. Truth is the foundation upon which all genuine understanding and meaningful existence are built. It is not only a possibility or an abstract concept but something that exists in fact, an unshakable reality that we are called to seek, embrace, and uphold in our lives. To live in truth is to walk in the light of what is real, concrete, and verifiable, rather than dwelling in the shadows of illusion or deception. In a world filled with uncertainties, falsehoods, and shifting narratives, the pursuit of truth becomes a real act of integrity and faith.

At the heart of this pursuit stands Yahweh, the divine Name that signifies Yahweh in the Scriptures. Yahweh is always associated with truth. He embodies the very essence of what is real and unchangeable. In the biblical context, Yahweh is described as "the God Yahweh of truth," a righteous and faithful Creator who cannot lie or be deceived. His Word is truth, and His promises are sure. When we acknowledge Yahweh as the one who stands for truth, we recognize that our relationship with Him is rooted in honesty and sincerity. Yahweh's nature calls us to reflect His character by walking in truth ourselves.

To walk in truth is to live with honesty before Yahweh and others. It means aligning our words, actions, and intentions with what is real and right. It requires humility to admit our faults, courage to stand firm in our convictions, and perseverance to pursue what is true despite challenges or opposition. This journey is not always easy, for truth often confronts comfort zones and shallow appearances. Yet, it is in these moments that our commitment to truth is tested and refined. Moreover, walking in truth is integral to our spiritual growth and moral integrity. When we embrace the truth about ourselves such as our weaknesses, flaws, and sins, we open the door to genuine repentance and changeover. When we accept the truth about the world around us, we can navigate life's complexities with wisdom and discernment. And when we uphold truth in our dealings with others, we advocate trust, respect, and genuine relationships.

Living in truth also means trusting in the reliability of Yahweh's Word and His promises. Yahweh's truth is steadfast and eternal. His commitments do not waver with circumstances or changing tides. As Yahweh's followers, we are called to anchor our lives in this unshakable truth, allowing it to shape our worldview, ethics, and daily choices. In doing so, we not only honor Yahweh but also embody the truth that can set others free from deception and confusion.

In a broader sense, truth is a divine gift and a reflection of the very nature of Yahweh himself. To walk in truth is to mirror divine integrity and to participate in the divine purpose of bringing clarity, justice, and love into the world. It is a sincere acknowledgment that reality matters deeply and that our actions should be rooted in what is real rather than what is convenient or false.

Truth is not a mere possibility. It is an existing, tangible reality that we are called to recognize and live out. Yahweh's divine nature as the embodiment of truth, invites us to do the same and to walk honestly, faithfully, and sincerely in all aspects of life. By aligning ourselves with this divine truth, we find purpose, peace, and authenticity. Let us, therefore, commit ourselves daily to the pursuit of truth, knowing that in doing so, we honor Yahweh and contribute to bringing His light into a world desperately in need of genuine truth. Now, on to the word "authenticity". It's a word that resonates deeply within the human heart. We all long to be seen for who we truly are flaws, imperfections, strengths, and all. In a world that often encourages masks and façades, the desire to be genuine remains a quiet but persistent longing. When it comes to our relationship with Yahweh, the Creator of all, this longing takes on an even more profound significance. Yahweh desires authenticity in His followers, not fake gestures or hollow words, but hearts that are honest and real before Him. From the very beginning, Yahweh has sought genuine people in His kingdom. Throughout scripture, we see time and again that Yahweh is drawn to sincerity rather than pretense. When Adam and Eve hid themselves after their downfall, Yahweh's first pursuit was to seek their hearts, call them out of hiding, and into an honest relationship. This demonstrates that Yahweh values truthfulness and clarity. Yahweh desires His people to come before Him with open hearts, devoid of charades, acknowledging their true selves and their need for His mercy.

Yahweh's desire for authenticity is beautifully exemplified in the life of King David. David was called "a man after Yahweh's own heart," not because he was perfect, but because he was honest about his flaws and sins. When David sinned, he didn't hide or deny his mistakes. Instead, he humbled himself, confessed, and sought forgiveness. His genuine repentance and heartfelt worship made him a person Yahweh could trust and love deeply. David's life teaches us that Yahweh values a sincere heart more than fake practices. Yahweh looks beyond outward appearances and seeks genuine devotion rooted in truth. Furthermore, Yahweh emphasizes the importance of truth. The Pharisees and religious leaders were often challenged for their hypocrisy and superficial piety. Yahweh emphasized that true worship is not about outward appearances or rituals alone but about heartfelt love and sincerity. For instance, see Case Law **§ Matthew 15:8-9**, a quote from Isaiah, saying, "These people honor me with their lips, but their hearts are far from me." He taught that Yahweh looks at the heart; He desires genuine worship that stems from love, humility, and truth. Those who approach Yahweh with honesty and humility find favor, for He values genuineness over empty practices. Yahweh's kingdom is not a place for pretense or false appearances. He invites us to be genuine, to bring our whole selves like our doubts, fears, weaknesses, and strengths, and lay them before Him. In doing so, we open ourselves to Yahweh's transformative power. Genuine people are humble enough to recognize their need for mercy, honest enough to admit their faults, and sincere enough to seek a deeper relationship with Yahweh. Such hearts are the ones Yahweh delights in, for they reflect His own desire for honesty and integrity. Living truthfully in our walk with Yahweh also means aligning our words and actions with our true beliefs and feelings. It involves being honest in prayer, sincere in worship, and transparent in our daily lives. It's about integrity and being who we truly are in every moment, no matter the circumstances. This truth encourages a deeper intimacy with Yahweh, allowing His love to penetrate the parts of us that are often hidden behind masks. Yahweh wants genuine people in His kingdom; Those who approach Him with sincere hearts, honesty, and humility. Yahweh is drawn to factuality because it reflects His own truth and love.

As followers of Yahweh, our goal should be to promote hearts that are real, clear, and fully devoted to Him. In doing so, we not only honor Yahweh but also experience the transformative power of His mercy, becoming more like Yahweh each day. Let us endeavor to be truthful in our walk, knowing that in our honesty, we find His love, mercy, and eternal presence. The word innocent carries a gentle reminder for us all. It is a quality that goes beyond mere lack of guilt; It embodies honesty, purity, and sincerity in our interactions with others. When we approach each person with genuine kindness and openness, we honor a deeper truth about ourselves and about the divine presence that guides us.

Being sincere in how we deal with each other is more than just good manners. It reflects our respect for the divine. In the Bible, it is often emphasized that our actions and words should be heartfelt and truthful, for in doing so, we mirror Yahweh's own honesty and goodness. When we are honest, we create trust and teach a sense of safety and peace in our communities.

Innocence also reminds us to see each other with compassion and without pretense. It is not about naivety or ignorance, but about choosing clarity and humility. When we are sincere, we declare that we have nothing to hide, and that we value facts over appearances. This sincerity is a way of acknowledging the Divine in every spiritual aspect, recognizing that everyone is deserving of kindness and respect.

Ultimately, living with innocence and sincerity is a way of expressing our reverence for Yahweh. It is an act of faith to be genuine, to speak and act from the heart, and to treat others with honesty and dignity. By doing so, we not only uphold our integrity but also reflect the divine love that is at the core of our existence. Let us strive to carry this sincerity in our daily lives, knowing that in doing so, we honor the sacredness within ourselves and others. Shalom Aleichem.

References

1. The Holy Bible, King James Version. Cambridge Edition: 1769; King James Bible Online, 2024. www.kingjamesbibleonline.org.

2. Merriam-Webster Dictionary. An Encyclopedia Britannica Company Online, 2024. www.https://www.merriam-webster.com.

3. Oxford English Dictionary. (2024). "Relationship." in the Oxford English Dictionary online. Retrieved from https://www.oed.com.

4. King James Version with Apocrypha, American Edition (KJVAAE): King James Version 1611, spelling, punctuation and text formatting modernized by ABS in 1962; typesetting © 2010 American Bible Society. Online 2024. https://www.bible.com/bible/546/GEN.1.KJVAAE.

5. Strong, James. The New Strong's Expanded Exhaustive Concordance of the Bible. Red letter ed., online. Thomas Nelson, 2022. Retrieved from https://strongsconcordance.org/. Site design and coding © copyright 2022, Danny Carlton Strong's Exhaustive Concordance of the Bible is public domain.

About Me

Tamar Israel is an author dedicated to spreading the knowledge of Yahweh. She has written transformative works such as הוהי Knowledge of Equity and The Laws of הוהי, designed to guide readers toward just judgments and alignment with the 613 laws, statutes, judgments, and commandments Yahweh has instructed us to follow.

Her books serve as roadmaps for living a life of purpose, fulfillment, and enlightenment in a chaotic and confusing world.

Born in the Nation of Yahweh in Miami, Florida, Tamar was honored to be named by Yahweh Ben Yahweh and attended private school at Yahweh's Educational Center (YEC). Inspired by the desire to help others avoid unintentionally breaking Yahweh's laws, Tamar's first book was created as a study tool focused exclusively on these divine principles. Her works are unique, blending nonfiction with esoteric insights and offering a fresh perspective on timeless truths.

Tamar attended The Art Institute of Philadelphia for Computer Animation and has been a licensed Notary Public for over 19 years. With more than 17 years of experience in the healthcare industry, she continues to work while raising four beautiful children with her husband. Tamar's books reflect her deep passion for guiding others to live in harmony with the universal laws that connect us all. If you're interested in learning more about Tamar and her works, please visit her at the following website online www.lulu.com/spotlight/iamtamarisrael.com.